Sir George Farrar

Sir George Farrar, D.S.O., M.L.A.
President and Leader of the Transvaal Progressive Federation.

Andrew Watson

Grosvenor House
Publishing Limited

This book is published by
Grosvenor House Publishing Ltd
Link House
140 The Broadway, Tolworth, Surrey, KT6 7HT.
www.grosvenorhousepublishing.co.uk

A CIP record for this book
is available from the British Library

ISBN 978-1-80381-281-6

INTRODUCTION

This book is written primarily for the benefit of George' s great grandchildren and their descendants for whom George and Ella lived in a distant part of history. I am the only grandchild remaining. Of the six daughters only Helen Mabel (1894), Muriel Frances (1896) and my mother Ella Marguerite (1911) had children. Helen had Tids (1920), George (1921) and Mickey (1923). Muriel had James (1922), who became 7th Earl of Lonsdale, Anthony (1925) and Ann (1927). I am my mother's only child born in 1937. My father left to fight in the Second World war in Egypt when I was just 18 months old, never to return. He died less than 3 years after my parents had married.

I knew that my grandfather had been famous but until I retired from practising as a barrister, I was never curious to discover more about him. My mother was perhaps understandably, reluctant to dwell upon the past. As can be seen George played an important role in the formation of The Union of South Africa and was seldom out of the public eye. Sidney was the eldest of the four boys but George's drive and his lack of inhibition soon resulted in him becoming the natural leader. He had this gregariousness and ability to get on with people from different backgrounds combined with a positive desire to discover and overcome fresh challenges. He was a gifted athlete, rider and all round sportsman despite his diminutive frame. At various times he was pilloried by political opponents and by the press but he was never deterred from pursuing what he believed to be the right course. He made plenty of mistakes but the testimonials received upon his death demonstrate that he always had considerable credit in the bank of national and international opinion.

I worked for Anglo American Corporation for 5 years firstly in London and then in Johannesburg before being called to the Bar in 1966.

Market Square – Pietermaritzburg

SIR GEORGE FARRAR

CHAPTER 1

George Farrar was a human dynamo. From what we know there were few uneventful or restful days in his life. Salesman, athlete, entrepreneur, father of six daughters, mining magnate, politician, town planner, farmer and soldier; he was tried for high treason, condemned to death by hanging, knighted and made a baronet. He became a household name on the Rand and in the 1968 South African Dictionary of Biography has four columns to himself.

George Herbert Farrar was born in 1859, the third of four sons born to Dr Charles Farrar and Helen Howard. While the boys were still very young Helen divorced her husband and took her four sons back from Chatteris in Cambridgeshire to her home town of Bedford and reverted to her maiden name of Howard. In her opinion her husband did not devote enough commitment to his practice; he used to go hunting on Fridays! The older boys were all educated at Bedford Modern School. Only the youngest, Fred was accepted into the Grammar School. He went on to Oxford University and after graduating became ordained and later became a Headmaster of Elstow School and later Dean of Bedford. He wrote two books about Bedfordshire. For some reason at some point Percy was sent to school in Switzerland and from then onwards he was only ever happy in the mountains. He became a distinguished mountaineer. President of The Alpine Club, he equipped the first ever Everest expedition and has 2 mountains named after him. His wife Mary was the first woman to climb Mont Blanc. According to my aunt Muriel she was utterly fearless and at an advanced age lived alone in London throughout the blitz. Their much loved and only child Joey was tragically killed at Flanders in a double tragedy for the Farrar family for George's fatal accident came 10 days later.

[illegible]

CAPT. JOHN HAROLD FARRAR.

One of the bravest and most beloved of officers has fallen by the death of Capt. John Harold Farrar, 1st Northamptonshire Regiment. He was the only officer of our sadly stricken 1st Battalion who had gone through the war unscathed. He seemed to have a charmed life but the terrible Sunday morning struggle for the St. Aubers ridge saw the end to his gallant life. Capt. Farrar, who was 27 years of age, was the only son of Mrs. Farrar, of Milton Ernest House, Bedfordshire, and Capt. Farrar, D.S.O., nephew of Mr. Sidney H. Farrar, of Heatherwood, Ascot, and of Col. Sir George Farrar, D.S.O., now A.Q.M.G. to the Central Force operating in German South West Africa. He joined the old Northamptonshire Militia as second lieutenant in 1905. On the abolition of the Militia he transferred to the 3rd or Special Reserve Battalion. Upon the outbreak of war he transferred to the 1st Battalion, and on August 12th went with it to France, where it formed part of the First Division. He shared the fortunes of his battalion in the retreat from Mons, the battles of the Marne and the Aisne, the severe fighting in October and November to the north-east of Ypres where his division supported the hard-pressed 7th Division, as well as in other actions. He was promoted captain on October 27th, and was mentioned in despatches early this year. He was for some time acting Adjutant to the Battalion, and sent us several cheery letters thanking our readers for their gifts of smokes and comforts to his men. A splendid horseman, he was a familiar figure with the Oakley Hounds, and as a rider at local point-to-point meetings. How much he was respected and how sadly he will be missed, is indicated by the following letter the bereaved mother has received from Comp.-Sergt.-Major Lodge, "D" Co., 1st Northamptonshire Regiment: "To Mrs. Farrar.—I am more than sorry to write and tell you that our brave soldier officer, Capt. Farrar, was killed in action on the morning of May 9th at the hour of 5.40 a.m. He was shot through the heart, his death being instantaneous. I must tell you that he was one of the most popular and bravest of officers in the regiment, loved and respected by all ranks of his regiment. He received orders to advance. He then got up gave the order to the men in his company to advance, and it was at that time he met his death within one hundred yards of the enemy's trenches. I can assure you of the regiment's deepest sympathy in your great and sad loss."

Capt. John Harold Farrar (Joey)

There is no record as to how George fared at school but his mother said that he managed to cram his way through exams 'but his work was deplorable'; she added that one report described him as 'always a gentleman never a student'. This showed one day when she was shopping holding a small parcel and he was 6 years of age. He told her: 'It wouldn't look good when you have someone alongside who could carry it for you'. We know he excelled as an athlete both as runner and as long jumper.

Helen's father had started the Britannia Ironworks in Bedford and her brothers took it on. After leaving school at just 16 the older boys went to work as apprentices in their uncles' business. The business made agricultural and later mining machinery. Sidney qualified as a civil and mining engineer but George does not appear then to have had any qualifications although he is later described as a qualified engineer. The Howards had clearly seen the potential for their business in South Africa. In 1878 George and Sidney were sent out to promote the business from bases in East London and Port

George, in his late teens

Elizabeth. Percy would join them later. As a salesman George was required to visit farming communities and later the gold mines to promote the company Howard Brothers' products. This gave him the opportunity to see how they were run and their potential. It was also important for him to see how the mining machinery could be improved and adapted. Anthony Trollope recalls meeting him as an 18 year old boy selling or attempting to sell ploughs and reaping machines (what we would have called binders) in Pietermaritzberg. The business flourished over the subsequent six years no doubt in part due to the salesmanship and zeal of George.

Sidney and George

Percy on one of his mountains

Main Street from Market Square in Port Elizabeth in c. 1878
shortly after George's arrival. The old Howard Bros. building
is the third building on the left beneath the double cross

CHAPTER 2

George attended the Eastern Province Championships in Queenstown and competed in the mile, breaking the national record in a time which stood for twenty years. My aunt Helen told me that he challenged the fastest African to a match over a mile. There was much betting on the outcome and shortly before the start George was made aware that his opponent had been paid to lose. Shortly after the start his opponent fell over and so George fell over too. There was pandemonium and rioting in the stands. No Stewards enquiry in those days!

He is described as a small, dapper man with a keen interest in all forms of sport. A fine horseman, at some stage he won 2 steeplechases. He won the half mile 60 guinea challenge Cup 2 years running and was determined to win a third but despite 3 attempts he was defeated on each occasion by a man called Brown. He then took up Rugby and played for a number of years for Queenstown Swifts presumably at scrum half on account of his size. In 1972 at Ellis Park, where National Rugby games have taken place for many years a silver Cup presented by George Farrar in 1898 was discovered tucked away in an old store. I have seen a photograph of it and it is truly massive. He rowed bow for Zwartkop Rowing Club when they won the Grand Challenge Cup for coxed fours in May 1881 together with a prize of £150. What intrigued me most were the individual weights of the crew, which are recorded on the photograph. George weighed 9st. 7lbs, stroke just 10 stone, the heaviest member was 10st. 10lbs and the cox a diminutive 5st. 7lbs.

It is said that he played all games as though his life depended on it. In later life he would attempt feats of endurance probably unwise in one who was a chain smoker. On a mountaineering expedition at St. Moritz, he insisted on racing his guide to the top of the mountain and had to rest for a few days in order to recover from his exertions. On the final day of a hunting party of 10 days at a point when they were 8 miles from home, he challenged the other members of the party for a wager of £5 to a race home as a result of which he had to retire to bed for a week.

George and Ella's first home in Doornfontein and
George and Helen in the carriage

Head Office of ERPM in Simmonds Street

CHAPTER 3

In 1886 Sidney and George decided it was time to move. Gold had been discovered in 1884 but by now it was apparent that there were extensive reserves on the Witwatersrand. They persuaded the Howards to put money into a new gold mining venture to be called initially Howard, Farrar and co. but with George as the Chairman and Sidney's expertise as a mining engineer a vital cog. The initial venture centred on the goldfields around Barberton in the lowveld, an area then rife with malaria. In those days Barberton could only be reached from Lourenco Marques, so they took a boat round the coast from Port Elizabeth and travelled across country through Portuguese East Africa. They did not stay long. Conditions were too oppressive so they decided to switch their activities to the East Rand, an area which prior to then had only been exploited in a small way for coal and was described in one journal 'as valueless from a mining point of view'. Their journey from Barberton took 4 days with 4 changes of horse. One has to bear in mind the limitations of transport at the time. There would have been rail links to the major cities and ports but travel on dirt tracks by ox cart was obviously restrictive. Percy would later come to Johannesburg and join his brothers but he never liked South Africa and never settled. George was then 27.

The first mine to open was the Angelo mine. By now numerous claims had been registered in the Benoni and Boksburg area by what was then known as the H. F. Syndicate. I assumed that the H stood for Howard but actually it stood for Hanau. Perhaps the brothers had hoped that their uncles would invest in the business but then had second thoughts. Carl Hanau was 'closely associated with George Farrar from the early nineties' but I cannot find any more about him as the Dictionary of South African Biography has been updated and many of the European sounding names have been removed. Carl then owned a mine at Doornkop and it may be significant that Doornfontein is where George and Ella went to live after they were first married and where Helen was born. It was a large bungalow with a white veranda running along the front and down both sides. It is not clear how many members belonged to the syndicate or who they were. I can only assume that Carl and maybe others were responsible for providing the bulk of the capital to purchase farms and register numerous claims in Benoni, Boksburg and surrounding areas. An article in The Citizen in August 1903 on The Farrar Group states: 'The Angelo was the first mine to get to work, and it was due to Sir George Farrar's indomitable perseverance and enterprise that single handed, he found the cash required to bring this mine into the producing stage, when as yet he could look nowhere for support'.

This assertion leaves huge question marks in my mind. Even in those days this enterprise required substantial capital and considerable expertise. Prospecting for gold and evaluating and assaying the quality and depth of the seams found were complex operations for which both brothers particularly George were singularly ill equipped. Sinking bore holes, establishing rail links and employing experienced technicians would each require major capital sums. They had no money of their own. A solicitor friend later revealed that when George left Port Elizabeth, he had exactly £200 to his name. Were the Howards really prepared to back their nephews in this venture after they had abandoned the family business in East London and Port Elizabeth, no doubt causing problems there? Maybe they could supply at least some of the necessary machinery with delayed payments or for a share but would they really have gone further? With the boys' credentials no bank is likely to have been more amenable. Only George and probably Carl Hanau know the answer to that question. A partial answer lies in the number of bondholders and preference shares which were issued.

The other unresolved and critical issue is what alerted them to the existence of gold reefs in the East Rand in the first place? Obviously, there were good reasons for concealing the answer to that question in the early years but did nobody discover in the years much later? Prospectors had been searching for gold all along the High Veldt.

How had they missed it when coal had been found so close by? Speaking after George's death Carl Hanau said: 'Sir George conferred an enormous boon on prospectors throughout the whole district known as the East Rand, which in those days when the Syndicate was formed, was practically given up as valueless ground from a mining point of view. The Syndicate was the first to back up their personal belief in the main reef of the Eastern series by hard work and very big money expenditure,' leaving the two intriguing questions posed above totally unanswered.

In due course East Rand Consolidated was formed and viable claims were sold to the company, who would be responsible for the mining operation. It is easy to see how George as a major shareholder in both operations became an extremely wealthy man in a remarkably short space of time.

At some time in the nineties the Farrar group as it was then known merged with or took over the Anglo-French Exploration Company, which as its name suggests was primarily a prospecting company but which owned a substantial amount of land in Rhodesia, including 358,000 acres in Matabeleland. How was this acquired one has to wonder. It is worth noting that whilst George must have acquired some knowledge of mining techniques and solving the many problems of mining underground, his real love lay in the countryside and in farming. The farm that he developed around Benoni and called Bedford farm, under his direction became a show farm and an example of how a farm could be successfully managed on the High Veldt. From the age of 18 he had been engaged with the farming community in Natal and the Eastern Cape. Following his death, the Farmer's Weekly reported on the sale of his entire Friesland herd by private auction on the Farm at Bedford. Despite the fact that it was in time of war, there was considerable attendance of buyers and experts from every province and the stock fetched record prices averaging £118 per head. £310 was paid for a milking cow, which had won competitions at Bloemfontein and Johannesburg. Marten Mulder, a well known authority on Frieslands writes: 'Bearing in mind the great attention of the late baronet to the selection of his animals it is not surprising that breeders of such importance went beyond their price limits knowing that these were animals Sir George would never have parted with in his lifetime. In his selection and in the constitution of his Friesland herd he was guided by others but gradually as he became more interested in the breed he ventured in accordance with his own opinions. He procured animals which were considered to be of deep milking strain and he despised of bulls which produced too much of a beef type. Under his influence the character of the herd changed over the years. He discarded heavy, tubby bulls for those with a more streamlined French formation and with cows he went for stronger animals whose constitutions were more resistant to TB. Though years and generations may pass and his name be forgotten the great good he has done to South Africa by his importation of valuable animals will live forever .... You could go all over the Netherlands and not find a herd as was represented on the day of the sale'.

'Sir George was a member of the Witwatersrand Dairy Farmers' Association and he took a keen interest in connection with dairying on the Rand. He came with us to Pretoria where he sought to obtain compensation for tuberculosis. He gave us valuable assistance and made the important speech'.

One of his farm managers recorded: 'Whenever Sir George comes around the farm with me, he always sees six times more than I do. Problems were never shelved; they were solved if necessary by calling in an expert in the field even on one occasion writing to an expert in the UK'.

By 1902 the Farrar group comprised 3 working gold mines, 1 coal mine and 15 prospecting companies, a number of farms and one township. East Rand Proprietary was by now quoted on the London Stock Exchange and in September of that year reached a high of £10 5/16. There were 975,000 issued shares of £1 each and George was the largest shareholder. The share price would never be as high again.

In a letter written by Percy dated 31st May 1918 addressed to Ella 3 years after George's fatal accident, he informs her of his discovery that the Board had voted without alerting any shareholders in advance of their decision to discontinue mining operations. Percy added that he and Patrick Duncan, who was the sole executor of George's will, had both been kept in the dark. Patrick Duncan was Resident Commissioner of Basutoland and later in 1937 was made the sixth Governor General of The Union of South Africa. Percy was particularly angry with a man called Gau, who was Percy's own nominee on the Board specifically to look after the interests of The Farrar Estate which was a major shareholder. Percy pointed out that only about a quarter of the claims had been worked out and something like 2,000 to 2,500 of the deeper level claims remained untouched. He felt that the Board's decision, which had of course caused a sharp fall in the share price, was totally unjustified. He sent an urgent cable to the Board asking for delay and within 24 hours managed to persuade two significant Board members namely Lionel Phillips and Lord Milner to co-sign a 7 page letter detailing a counter proposal. Percy pointed out that the gold price was currently high and that there were sufficient cash reserves of £500,000 to finance drilling to the lower levels in order to evaluate the richness of the seams at those levels. Sadly, but perhaps predictably it fell upon deaf ears. The bugbear was the debenture debt, which then stood at £920,000. This was clearly the source of the initial financing solving one of the mysteries outlined above. The price had fallen to 3/ 9d. Percy sold his shares at that price and urged Ella to sell as many as she could. Presumably she did because at her death in 1922 there were none in her estate. When I joined Anglo American in 1958 the share price was quoted in pence and the seams were believed to be almost exhausted. I was very surprised to read that the mine remains active today and has become the second deepest mine in the world. The main reef is mined at a depth of 3,200 metres, just 100 metres above Western Deep Levels in The Orange Free State. The company was purchased in October 2002 by Crown Gold Recoveries and is now a wholly owned subsidiary of DRDGOLD SA. Gold production totalled 82,850 ounces in the latest year's accounts and the shares were quoted at 5p but now, 4 months later, they are 47p. This is the same mine that George Farrar discovered by accident and created more than 120 years ago! George would remain Chairman of the company until his death in 1915.

CHAPTER 4

In 1893 George now 34 married Ella Mabel Waylen then about 24 in Johannesburg. Had the marriage taken place in England that bare statement from the records would strongly indicate that the marriage took place in a Registry Office otherwise the church would have been identified.

It is hard to believe that Ella enjoyed a very happy childhood. She was the fourth of 8 children born to Charles William Waylen and Eliza Jane Mcintosh. Two of her siblings died in the year of their birth. Apart from Ella and her older brother Frank, none of the other children's deaths are recorded.

I say that she was 'about' 24 in 1893 because only the first two children's births were registered. We only know the age of the other children because of the ages attributed to them at the time of a census. It is possible that Ella may not have known the actual date of her birthday. This is underlined by a scrap of paper I have recently seen in the Farrar archives now lodged in The Weston Library (part of The Bodleian). It records the birth dates of all members of the family but against Ella's name 'Jan' has been deleted and 'September' substituted and then '27' is added whereas in all other cases the date precedes the month suggesting that the date may have been added. At the time of Ella's birth her mother, Eliza, was lawfully married to Arthur Tulloch, who had issued divorce proceedings citing her father Charles as Co Respondent. At the time of her birth her father was employed in the Indian Army's medical service. His father and grandfather were also in the medical profession. Subsequently her father brought her mother and the 6 children to London, where he obtained work at what was then the South Eastern Fever Hospital and much later became New Cross Hospital. In September 1874 he married her mother in London. At the time he was described as a Medical Superintendent. 10 years later he is described as a surgeon.

Photograph of Ella before she met George

Before 1881 he deserted the family. At that time they were living in Chelsea. He had an address in Graston Road, which is close to Chalk Farm. That is in 1881 when Ella was 11 or 12.

I have discovered that Ella first met George on the boat when travelling to South Africa with one of her sisters and had been in Johannesburg for about 2 years before she married George and that she had been on the stage either in Johannesburg or in London or possibly both. I discovered this because some time, perhaps long after Bedford Farm was completed, George commissioned Sir Herbert Baker to design a theatre in End St. Doornfontein for his 'musically and theatrically accomplished wife and daughter Gwen'. The building is still standing and was in 1967 reopened as the Adam Leslie Theatre. It is a lovely typical Herbert Baker building but has had a chequered history. It has been an engineering workshop and a spaghetti factory. Adam Leslie, an entrepreneur, recalls having seen Gwen performing with her partner Nora Blaney at Golders' Green Hippodrome wearing tango boots and a black fringe. 'She hasn't much of a voice but she is a natural comedienne'.

She and George were probably used to surprising other people and may for different reasons have represented exactly what the other was looking for. As one can see from photographs and pictures, Ella cut a striking figure and is unlikely to have been too demanding having discovered someone, who was genuinely fond of her and could take care of her. Ella managed to establish a good relationship with George's mother, which cannot have been easy, even naming her firstborn after her. I can think of a few brides who would have jibbed at that. As far as we can tell she and George remained devoted for the whole of their lives. Of course it maybe that she looked upon Helen as the mother she would like to have had and confided in her.

Before Ella met George she was referred to as 'a darling of Johannesburg society'. She had then described herself as 'a member of a northern counties' family'. This puzzled me until I discovered that her mother had taken the entire family to Northern Ireland where, according to Ella, they lived on a diet of milk and potatoes and clearly survived in very straightened circumstances. Quite how

Ella eased herself apparently effortlessly into Johannesburg society in such a short time after having left Northern Ireland remains something of a mystery. She had natural poise and an hourglass figure, which we can see in early photographs. When my mother died in 1985, we opened a tin trunk, which had clearly never been opened since her mother's death in 1922. It contained clothes including her wedding dress which had specks of blood where the corset bones had dug into her ribs demonstrating the agonies women of that era suffered to maintain their figure. Also in the trunk were 2 letters from Basil Blackwood. Both are illustrated one with a picture of him kneeling on the platform of Bloemfontein station as she passes through on The Blue train.

Basil Blackwood was the third son and fifth child of the first Marquess of Dufferin and Ava. He was born in Ireland but spent much of his childhood in Canada where his father was Governor General. He went to Harrow school and went up to Balliol College in 1891 aged 21 but never graduated. At Balliol Hilaire Belloc became his best friend. In due course HB invited him to illustrate his first book of humorous children's verse 'The Bad Child's book of Beasts' and thereafter he illustrated all of HB's books. He was called to the bar in 1896 and in 1901 handpicked by Lord Milner, then High Commissioner of South Africa to form part of his 'Kindergarten'. As far as I can deduce the object was to present a softer kinder face to counteract memories of the brutality of Kitchener's regime. He was put in charge of The Judge Advocate's department in Bloemfontein, which I imagine would have required him to speak Afrikaans fluently. He was also made Assistant Colonial Secretary of the Orange Free State, which post he held for 6 years until 1907. At the outbreak of war in 1914 he signed up and obtained a commission in the 9th Lancers at the age of 44. He served as a 'galloper' at the battle of Mons and was severely wounded on October 14th and returned to the UK. While unfit for active service he enrolled in and served in the Intelligence Corps. He was killed in action in the course of a night raid at Boesinghe near Ypres by which time he had transferred to The Grenadier Guards. His name is inscribed on the Menin Gate Memorial to the Missing. Muriel describes him as one of her mother's most devoted admirers. She quotes another letter from him which strongly suggests that although she obviously enjoyed his company, she managed to keep him at arm's length. 'My innings anyway is done. I'm out clean bowled without a run'. As you can see, he managed to ruin her visitors' book by covering it with his drawings. She must surely have shed a tear when news of his death came through so soon after that of George.

Ella was musical, regularly giving concerts with and without her 3 eldest children on The Union Castle Line to entertain passengers to and from South Africa. She painted to a reasonably high standard and was obviously fun to be with. On occasions she deputised for George on the hustings so she was clearly not lacking in self-confidence. I have read a speech she delivered in Bedford to open a concert at the beginning of The First world war to raise money for the troops. It is extremely well composed.

One of Basil Blackwood's caricatures

Painting of the façade of Bedford Farm by Ella

Guests at Bedford Farm

Ella, with her first-born daughter, Helen, 1894

CHAPTER 5

Until he controversially imported Chinese workers, George had employed mainly British and Africans in the mines and was in the vanguard of those advocating the rights of Uitlanders. The Reform Party, of which George became Chairman, sought to put pressure on Paul Kruger, the President of the South African Republic, which then comprised the whole of the Transvaal, to give full political rights to those who had left Europe and America to make their fortunes in the South African Goldfields, the majority of which lay in the Transvaal. At that time South Africa was roughly divided into four. The two British colonies The Cape Colony and Natal and the two Boer Republics the Orange Free State and the Transvaal. This situation came about as a consequence of the First Boer War. Without going over the history of South Africa it will suffice to say that from 1877 the Transvaal had been governed and administered by the British from Pretoria but to the accompaniment of seething Boer resentment. This resentment was occasioned almost entirely by the British treatment of the slave trade. Prior to the British invasion of The Cape in 1795 the Dutch East India Company had imported slaves from Malaysia (then known as Jakarta), Angola, Guinea and Mozambique. In 1807 the British passed The Slave Trade Act prohibiting any external slave trade and at the same time passed Amelioration Acts designed to improve the living conditions for slaves. These allowed slaves to marry, purchase their own freedom, live with their families and receive a basic education. No British settler arriving after 1820 was permitted to own a slave. On 1st January 1834 slavery was abolished in its entirety. This resulted in a massive trek out of Cape Colony into The Orange Free State for the majority of Boers then living in The Cape Colony. Not only had the British taken control of the land they believed to be their land but they had destroyed their way of living forcing them to move.

The First Boer War lasted just 3 months from the 16th December 1879 to the 23rd March 1880 and resulted in a humiliating defeat for the British and was a remarkable strategic and tactical success for Paul Kruger personally. Under his leadership, in each of the principal strongholds the army garrisons were placed under siege. The Boer Commandos were an expert light cavalry, which relied on camouflage, mobility, stealth and remarkable marksmanship. When supplies were almost exhausted, PK offered the British Government peace terms. Unnerved by the numbers of casualties particularly those of senior officers, Prime Minister Gladstone accepted them. Thus was the Transvaal created a Boer Republic. Bear in mind that George had arrived in Cape Town just 6 months before these events took place.

'Uitlanders' is a Dutch term meaning 'foreigners' or outsiders. Most of them were British but there were some Americans and other Europeans. Their principal grievance was that they were not entitled to become a citizen and obtain the vote unless they originated from Holland. President Kruger felt that it was a privilege which only he could grant. Some exceptions were made but only after the individual had lived continuously in the Transvaal for 15 years and done nothing to disturb the President. In addition, high taxes were being imposed by the Government on gold produced and on dynamite sold. Dynamite was necessary for blasting boreholes and following the seams underground and for laying railway lines. The Uitlanders also felt that they were providing the vast bulk of the funds being used to administer the State and felt they should have some say in how those funds were being utilised. A further significant bone of contention lay in the way in which the main Cape Town to Johannesburg railway line was being administered by the Transvaal Government. The line had been built by the British. More than two thirds of the line lay within the Cape Colony. The Transvaal Government imposed heavy tariffs on all freight as soon as it entered the Transvaal. In order to circumvent this, industrialists and mine owners arranged that their freight was unloaded before crossing the Vaal River and travelled the remainder of the journey by road. The Boer response was to close the road to heavy traffic at the commencement of the Vaal Drifts.

CHAPTER 6

Paul Kruger genuinely feared that the Uitlanders, estimated at one point as 600,000, might outnumber the Boers. Others felt this was unrealistic but even if it was, he certainly didn't want a repeat of what had occurred at Kimberley upon the finding of diamonds. 10,000 British settlers ejected Transvaal administrators and annexed this part of what had been part of the Orange Free State and held it by force declaring it to be the Klipdrift republic, before it became a separate British Crown colony under its original name of Griqualand West.

George took a leading role in the insurgency leading up to the 'Jameson Raid' by importing rifles hidden in crates into the mines he owned at Benoni and Boksburg.

Sir Leander Starr Jameson, a hitherto mild-mannered Administrator General of Matabeleland and a close associate of Cecil Rhodes, then Prime Minister of The Cape Colony, proposed to march via Bechuanaland with 400 mounted police and 200 foot soldiers. The Reform Committee of which George was a leading member would organise resistance and storm the armoury in Pretoria.

Joseph Chamberlain, the Colonial Secretary was made aware of the general nature of the plan and 'entirely off the record' lent his support. Before lending this support, he had apparently been advised that the greatest threat to British rule was not war with Kruger but peace between the English and the Afrikaners! Until confronted by some written evidence in the form of cablegrams, Chamberlain had steadfastly denied lending support.

There seems little doubt that Cecil Rhodes would have briefed Jameson and encouraged him to participate in this venture because he wanted the mineral wealth of the Transvaal to be under British control.

Sensing the heightened tensions Paul Kruger sent two prominent members of the Volksraad, Malan and Marais as peace envoys to meet the Reform Committee. They met at the Consolidated Goldfields' offices in Johannesburg (Chairman: Lionel Phillips). George arrived late with his shirtsleeves rolled up and his arms smeared with oil as the peace envoys were addressing the meeting. Clearly believing this might impress them he apologised for his lateness explaining that he had been busy for some hours unpacking rifles! After the meeting he expressed the surprisingly sanguine opinion that the meeting had gone well and that he was convinced that Paul Kruger could be persuaded to meet the Uitlanders' grievances. I suppose that the mere sending of envoys demonstrated that Kruger may have been looking for a way of easing tensions but the Committee never seems to have tabulated a list of demands and the envoys will have left with the implicit if not explicit threat of violence. Apart from anything else history demonstrated that Afrikaners felt far more deep-rooted grievances against the British and did not react well to being threatened.

During this period there were many communications between Chamberlain and the Pretoria Government and Paul Kruger appointed a Commission to investigate the Uitlanders' complaints. It comprised Chief Justice Kotze, Mr Justice Ameshof and Mr. Kock. On the 1st January they met The Reform Committee comprising Lionel Phillips, George Farrar, Col. Frank Rhodes (brother of Cecil) and John Hays Hammond and possibly the Secretary Percy Fitzpatrick (author of 'Jock of the Bushveld'). There is no record of what was said at this meeting, but it is worth pointing out that Jameson and his 'army' had already set out from Matabeleland 2 days previously.

What is clear is that by sheer force of personality George had made himself the chief spokesman for the Committee but by no means all Uitlanders supported their actions. At a public meeting in Boksburg very close to one of George's own mines and which must have included some of his own employees, it was decided that they did not want war with Kruger (see 'Past and Present' by Deryck Humphriss, a Bedford man, who attended George's old school

Bedford Modern) and it may have been this which caused George to waver. It is alleged that he informed Jameson that the raid was to be called off (presumably having consulted the other members of the Committee). It is not at all clear where Jameson was at this point. There never was an agreed plan because Cecil Rhodes and Jameson (although he would later deny this) wanted total surrender of power whereas the Reform Committee would be content if Kruger stepped down and was replaced by his Finance Minister, Lucas Meyer, whom they thought better understood their grievances.

Derrick Humphriss describes Jameson as a 'man who believed he was born under a lucky star' and that he could 'add the wealth of Johannesburg to the expanding British Empire with a bold stroke of bravado'. Others too may have seen him in this light but it does not give the whole picture. When well embarked on a successful medical career as house physician, house surgeon and demonstrator of anatomy at University College Hospital in London he suffered a nervous breakdown from overwork.

Jameson set out for Africa with mixed motives no doubt one of which will have been a sense of adventure but intending to practise medicine under less stress in a place where his skills were needed and would be more appreciated. In fact his repute spread quickly after his arrival at Kimberley. Paul Kruger, the man against whom the Jameson Raid was directed was one of his patients! Lobengula king of the Ndebele, made up of Zulus, who had fled north to Matabeleland following one of the Zulu wars, was another client whom he cured of gout. Lobengula was so grateful that he made him an induna (tribal chief), possibly the only white man to be so appointed. Later he introduced Cecil Rhodes to Lobengula. Rhodes and Jameson promised Lobengula money and weapons on an undertaking that he would not sell concessions to any Boers or Portuguese. Some of Lobengula's tribesmen took part in the Jameson Raid under Jameson's command. Jameson had no military training whatsoever. Others describe him as a natural leader with an abundance of charm. In his autobiography Rudyard Kipling revealed that he wrote his poem 'If' with Leander Jameson in mind.

George is often described as a shrewd operator; it was an uncharacteristic lapse of judgment to lend his name to this escapade, which appears to have had no clear plans as to what they would do even if it had been successful. Muriel believed that her mother did not want George to join the Reform Committee and that Ella had gone to try to dissuade Cecil Rhodes from launching an attack on the Transvaal, but she does not reveal how she discovered this.

Jameson was under instructions to wait in Bechuanaland until he received further information from the Committee as to the position in Johannesburg and Pretoria. No message had been received from the Reform Committee probably because Jameson's men had cut the wrong telephone wires. On 29th January 1895 the troops were becoming impatient and Jameson gave the order to proceed. Pretoria had been made aware of their advance not long after they left Bechuanaland. There were some preliminary skirmishes but they proceeded with only minor losses until they reached Krugersdorp, where they came under sustained attack. The Boer Commandoes had installed a roadblock. Jameson retreated and found a way round but they were eventually forced to surrender at Doornkop (the site incidentally of Carl Hanau's own mine) situated some 18 miles from Johannesburg. They were exhausted having been on the march for the better part of 3 days. 17 men were killed and 55 wounded. It is not at all clear to me what happened then. Obviously they would have been disarmed and Jameson and other officers taken to Pretoria and imprisoned. A Major White had in his despatch box, together with other incriminating evidence, the fateful letter of invitation bearing the signatures of George Farrar, John Hays Hammond, Lionel Phillips and Frank (brother of Cecil) Rhodes about his person. They were rounded up together with 60 other supporters. Reports say that the British non-residents, which constituted the majority of the raiders, were released to the British to be tried by them. Jameson himself would be tried in London for 'Organising an illegal expedition into the territory of a friendly state'. In certain parts of the British press there was strong anti Boer feeling and Jameson was portrayed as a hero. The defence was that the expedition had the full support of the Colonial Secretary and therefore could not be considered a criminal enterprise. Because Cecil Rhodes refused to disclose the cablegrams that had passed between him and Chamberlain that defence had to be withdrawn from the jury there being no evidence to support it. He was in due course found guilty and sentenced to 15 months without hard labour. An appeal that this failure to disclose rendered the trial unfair resulted in a Queen's pardon, the then Prime Minister Lord Salisbury having been forced to reveal the tenor of cables passing between Cecil Rhodes and Joseph Chamberlain. Cecil Rhodes was forced to resign his post as Prime Minister of The Cape Colony and 18 months later Dr Leander Jameson was elected Prime Minister in his place!

Interestingly in a later speech in Pietermaritzberg the Natal Advertiser quotes Dr Jameson as having said that the purpose of the raid was to make Lucas Meyer President; they had never wanted to overturn the Transvaal Government. He described the principal issues as exorbitant freight charges and the closure of the Vaal River drifts. Cynics would point out that that is not how Cecil Rhodes and Joseph Chamberlain saw it.

It does not seem as though anyone else was put on trial in the United Kingdom or in either of the South African colonies.

One has to ask why Kruger chose to release Jameson. Did they consider that as a non-resident he could not be tried for high treason? There was clear evidence for a charge of conspiracy. Was it because Kruger knew Jameson as his erstwhile Doctor? Was Jameson interrogated? It would surely be remarkable if he was not. Was he offered this deal if he provided credible evidence with regard to the organisers? The answer to these and many other questions may well lie in a detailed autobiography (two fat volumes which were published in London in English) written by Kruger after he had fled to Switzerland, before his death.

The signatories and 60 of their supporters were rounded up and placed in gaol in Pretoria and charged with treason. Shortly before his arrest George sent a characteristically breezy cable to Ella, who with baby Helen had been despatched to England to stay with his mother, which she or her daughter in law later had bound in an

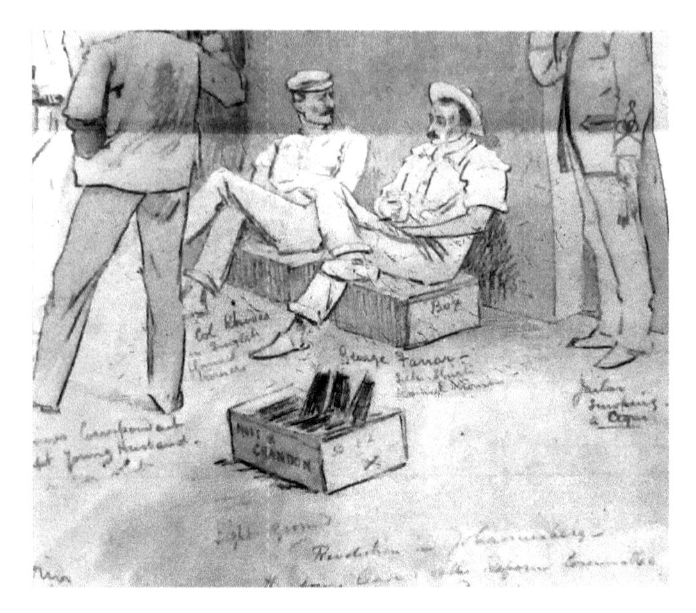

Life inside the prison cell

album of all the cables received at this time. It reads 10th January 1996: 'All well here. Think I may be about to be arrested. Will be pure formality. Probably token fine'. The tone of subsequent cables mainly from Percy grows gradually more sombre. 28th January: 'George spirits and fortitude unruffled. Severe sentence always possible. Rely confident on President's clemency'. 'Sidney says even if severest sentence it will be commuted. Keep up courage'. Finally, 'News very bad. Death recommendation'. 'Tell mother George bore himself like a man. She may well be proud of him'. There were a number of complaints about the conditions. But none from George.

They were placed in the same cell 12 feet square without any conveniences. The cells had previously been used only for native African prisoners and they were all bitten by bugs. Other prisoners were placed in even smaller cells with 4-5 in a cell. At some point the prison doctor intervened and they were given more space. The prison Governor Du Plessis was said to be related to Kruger in some way but he turned out to be a genial sort, allowing the prisoners to receive food parcels from family to supplement the mealie meal pulp they would otherwise be required to eat with their fingers. When Hammond Hayes was clearly suffering, he was allowed to move to secure accommodation nearby. Hammond Hayes was an American, said to be the most respected mining engineer in the world.

Kruger assigned Judge Gregorowski to try the signatories and 60 of their supporters. There was a legitimate objection to his appointment because he came from the Orange Free State and therefore had no legal standing in the Transvaal but this objection was overruled. The problem was that some of the other senior judges recused themselves mainly because they had made public statements which would have prevented them conducting a fair trial. Mr Justice Morrice had Scottish ancestry and it was feared he might have sympathies for the Defendants. There were certainly no such fears where Gregorowski was concerned. He had a record of particularly harsh sentences for non-Boers.

Aside from his signature there was a good deal of evidence against George. He had held public meetings to whip up feelings; he had helped to form irregular military units such as the Australian, Irish, Scottish and George Washington corps; he had imported large quantities of arms and ammunition. However, against most of the remainder there was little or no evidence. State Counsel, Dr Coster, sought to remedy this by calling on a preliminary enquiry, openly described by him as 'a fishing expedition'. He maintained that it was common practice in Holland although not in the Transvaal and was consistent with Roman Dutch law. Nobody felt able to contradict these assertions. This is not so surprising when one learns that he had recently completed all his legal training in Holland. He called first Mr Justice Ameshof and Chief Justice Kotze and elicited from them the names of those who attended the meeting on the 1st January and produced a list of supporters given to them by the Committee. It would certainly be very interesting to learn precisely what did transpire at that meeting but it seems we will never know.

Percy Fitzpatrick was used to taking minutes and he kept an extremely good record of the trial and preliminary hearing. If the Raid itself was a debacle the subsequent trial was an embarrassing farce. A kangaroo court would be far too polite a description.

Eddie Simpson was a solicitor practising in Pretoria whom George knew. He instructed J. Rose Innes QC the leader of the Bar in The Cape Colony to defend the Committee. Rose Innes had practised at the Pretoria Bar but he had not renewed his Practising Certificate 'and it was too late now'. Objection to his appearance was upheld. He remained for a while in an advisory capacity but his replacement was a hothead unwilling to take advice, called Wessels. He lost his temper when cross examining Chief Justice Kotze, who told him that what transpired between the Commission and the Reform Committee was privileged, which it almost certainly would have been. Both sides would have wanted a Without Prejudice discussion and certainly the Chief Justice would have made that clear. 'Oh! So, you are a judge who is willing to give evidence which might help the Government but unwilling to give evidence which might assist the Defendants'. If he knew anything of the law of privilege that was a pretty cheap shot; if he didn't it simply betrayed his ignorance however much short-term comfort it may have given Reform supporters in the public gallery. He certainly brought out the worst in his opponent. Dr Coster the State Attorney called as his second witness a Mr. Schumacher and proceeded to ask him about something called 'The Development Council' about which Schumacher seemed rather hazy. 'Well, what did you think it was?' The witness first said he didn't see how his thoughts could be relevant but later said that he couldn't now remember what he did think. Infuriated by this answer from his own witness the State Attorney then applied for the witness to be sent to the cells for 12 hours for contempt of court. Application granted! The witness then tried to appeal and 7 hours later his appeal was heard and overturned by de Korte J, who said that he had consulted Kotze CJ before making his ruling. Whereupon the State Attorney himself appealed again and this time Kotze CJ, who if you remember was a witness in the case himself, reversed the appeal and upheld the original ruling. Alice in Wonderland was looking on with bemusement. To onlookers and to the Defendants this was a clear demonstration that they could not expect a fair trial. It is important to try to understand the heightened tensions, which existed outside court particularly in Pretoria. The Volksteem in an article clearly designed to arouse feelings throughout the City, referred to householders in the Cape

Colony agreeing to have the beam in their house, upon which loyal brethren had been hung, removed for posterity and added to The National Museum in Pretoria. The article reported the arrival of the beam in Pretoria. After having described in detail the Slagter's Nek executions it called upon burghers (who would form the jury), to avenge on the Reformers their murdered countrymen. Upon arrival at Pretoria Station the Reformers required a mounted escort to protect them from the baying crowd, who lined the street to the Court.

Although the named members of the Committee had no defence to the charge of treason, they did have mitigation. If believed they had told Jameson not to proceed and attempted to call the raid off. They had not carried out their part of the agreement namely storming the armoury at Pretoria because they assumed Jameson would abide by their wishes. As far as George was concerned, he genuinely believed Kruger would negotiate their grievances. As far as The Uitlanders

Pretoria.

Sir,

Please see that the prisoners,

L. Phillips,

J. H. Hammond,

Col. F. Rhodes,

Geo. Farrar

are kept apart from the others, and be given no opportunity to speak to them.

Your Obedient Servant,

(sgd.) F. J. Coster,

S.A.

Notice forbidding contact with the other prisoners
signed by the chief Prosecutor at the trial

were concerned they were asking no more than what was conceded by all other Governments in South Africa namely that each person under reasonable conditions could become a citizen of the State. That on the 26th December not being able to contact Dr Jameson directly they despatched Major Heaney (by train via Kimberley) and Captain Holden across country to forbid any further movement on Dr Jameson's part. At the meeting of the 26th it was minuted that the Committee reiterates its desire to maintain the independence of the Republic and a copy of the minute was produced by Percy Fitzpatrick.

At the conclusion of the evidence an offer was made not to proceed against the majority (against whom there was no evidence) if the principals would plead guilty to treason. The majority felt such loyalty to the principals that they all refused this offer. The State Attorney agreed not to seek exemplary punishment and not to dispute any of the mitigating grounds, which were reduced to a written statement. But he did add that nothing he could say would be binding on the Judge. The principals felt the prospect of an acquittal was highly improbable and if found guilty by a jury it would be far more difficult for the President to exercise clemency in the aftermath so they each pleaded guilty. All ladies were required to leave court. The black cap, which Gregorowski had borrowed for the occasion was donned and the four were condemned to be executed by hanging.

What can Ella have been thinking? They had been married just under 2 years. She was pregnant with Muriel. It would appear that the President himself was genuinely taken aback by the sentences or that he feared the consequences if the sentences were carried out. The following day he agreed to be interviewed by the Press and announced that he would scratch the death sentence with immediate effect. His reason was that there was no vindictive feeling on his part or on the part of his government towards the prisoners. Reporting this the Times added their belief that at the conclusion of their sentence the principals would be banished for life and the remainder for a short time. It would certainly be very interesting to learn how Kruger's intervention was reported in the Volksteem. I have just seen a photograph which I think was probably taken the following day.

It shows Lionel Phillips and Frank Rhodes clearly drunk and barely able to stand in the prison yard outside the cell. George is leaning with his back to the wall between them. Inside the cell one can just see a woman whom I believe to be Lady Phillips, the same woman who had earlier complained most vociferously about the conditions in which they were being held, smoking a cigar! 26 days later, on the 26th May, their sentences were commuted to 15 years imprisonment followed by banishment. What were the supervening events, which lead to second thoughts? Did Kruger fear retaliation by the Uitlanders? Was there communication with the British Government? A fortnight later the Boers were prepared to be even more magnanimous and, on the 11th June, the Executive Council of the Pretoria Government (once again taking the matter out of the Judge's hands) quashed the sentence of imprisonment and substituted fines of £25,000 in each case. Cecil Rhodes paid his brother's fine and that of Lionel Phillips. Percy Farrar drew a cheque for the required sum and George was released the same day. My aunt Helen used to have the original cheque stub and the cheque itself is in one of the family files. After payment of the fine each man was required to sign an undertaking that in future they will neither directly nor indirectly interfere with the internal or external politics of the Republic and that they will conduct themselves as orderly and obedient inhabitants of the State. The threat of banishment was removed.

Following their release, The Times leader read: 'While we condemn the wholesale disenfranchisement of a capable and enterprising community, we can well understand the indignant feelings of Transvaalers against men who intrigued to overthrow their rule by secret, unscrupulous and indefensible methods'.

George publicly disowned Jameson and described him as a cad. What prompted this feeling? Was it purely because Jameson had persisted with the raid in defiance of the wishes of the Reform Committee or was there something more? After Gwen (George's third daughter) died in 1944 Jameson's daughter wrote to The Times to say that Gwen's father and her father had always been staunch allies yet in one of George's many obituaries H.G.Tibbutt wrote that following George's release from prison he refused to speak to

George taking Ella and Percy Fitzpatrick
to visit his cell many years later

Jameson for many years afterwards. Muriel recalls him being a regular visitor to Chicheley 12 years later.

More interestingly did George speak with Kruger, the man who had undoubtedly saved his life? Not as far as we can tell.

A few months later Mrs Hays Hammond revealed in the Women's section of The Sunday Times that not all his cellmates had enjoyed sharing a cell with George. He couldn't keep still and was forever tidying. Her husband complained that George had always washed up his mug before he had had his second mug of coffee. George chastised her for not having house trained her husband!

Following their release and their arrival back in Johannesburg Phillips and Farrar were carried shoulder high into The Stock Exchange amidst continued cheering and the building was invaded by an excited crowd notwithstanding the exertions of janitors to exclude unauthorised persons, reported the Johannesburg weekly Times.

I had always assumed that the Jameson raid was a major contributory factor to the outbreak of the Second Boer War, but in the intervening passage of nearly 4 years there were a number of other more immediate contributory factors not least actions of the British Government and inaction from the Transvaal Government and coercions from the Dutch Government and not least the somewhat blinkered English and Afrikaans press. The immediate effect of The Jameson raid was to put an end to any further consideration of the grievances outlined on behalf of the Uitlanders, but they did not suddenly disappear nor did Rhodes' desire for the mineral wealth of the Transvaal to be an imperial asset. Joseph Chamberlain clearly shared this desire and Rhodes and Chamberlain felt that Paul Kruger could be bullied. The knowledge that the conspirators said they would have been happy with Lucas Meyer as President would have put paid to any influence he might have had and the Uitlanders almost certainly had no other sympathisers in the Cabinet.

One might have expected some appreciation of Paul Kruger's magnanimity but writing 3 weeks after the principals had been released The Johannesburg weekly Times laid the blame for the Jameson raid squarely on the Government's shoulders: 'We detest a system of Government which appears at once stupid and despotic, unjust and short sighted ... BUT if relationships between South Africans have been put back 25 years to long forgotten disputes between Dutch and English the future looks grim ... these now threaten to break out into open warfare'. A few months later the same paper did a feature on George from which I quote 'He took his death sentence like a true Briton. When he and his fellow conspirators were released the majority of them rushed back to England in order to enjoy a good time to compensate for the horrors of Pretoria Prison. But Farrar was not that sort of man. He remained in Johannesburg to protect his shareholders' interests and to keep his very sharp eye on the mining industry. Under the rising South African financial sun there are few mining concerns in which he is not interested. He was and still is on many boards. There appears no limit to his ambition and progress ... The others were jealous of Farrar's success. He had that rare capacity for stirring up a person's enthusiasm and making it bubble'. Lionel Phillips would never return to South Africa.

CHAPTER 7

There seems little doubt that George was a control freak. As the cartoon on ERPM (East Rand Proprietary Mines) suggests, few decisions were made without George's personal authority. He liked to make regular unscheduled visits underground and throughout the mine and to engage individuals in conversation. Wherever he went he kept his eyes open. He wanted to hear any complaints from individual workers rather than from their union. Whether he ever spoke Afrikaans or Zulu or any other native language like his grandson George Turner I rather doubt. Mining has a special glossary of its own with English, perhaps with Yorkshire origins, and all written instructions would have been in this language. Native Africans would have been instructed in it. The word 'native' was defined in law in 1906 as 'any person both of whose parents belong to any aboriginal race or tribe of Africa'. Those of mixed race were defined as 'coloured', and this classification conferred advantages in terms of land tenure and parliamentary representation. Something like 90 % of Coloureds spoke Afrikaans as their first language indicating the main source of their mixed race.

George's control freakery was not restricted to the mine and the office. It filtered through into domestic arrangements and as you have seen even the prison cell. When Ella was away, he would write often describing detailed rearrangements of the household. Examples: 'Margaret was not looking very well. She has trouble at home so I have given her the day off'. 'They spend far too long on their own laundry so I have arranged that it be sent to an outside laundry so that they can do more productive work here'. In another letter written to Ella in 1910 George wrote: 'The country will never go ahead until we face the issue of the coloured man and the colour bar. Today we employ a tremendous lot of natives and educate them year by year to become better workmen but by the colour bar they are all tied down to one level. We have thousands of boys who could do excellent work on their own account even blasting but by the colour bar we are not allowed to use them ... It will in truth be a case of India all over again. When you have trained and educated the native you slam the door of industrial opportunity against them. That is by preventing them from doing anything but rough unskilled work ... I am quite certain that if the colour bar were removed natives would do a great deal of work which white men are doing now. This will come in time and of course it means a tremendous social upheaval'. He cannot have believed that it would be another 75 years before it happened. He carried out Time and Motion studies on the mine and discovered that the African did 50% more work than the white man in an average shift but made 10% more mistakes. The Chinese did 25% more work than a white man but made 20% more mistakes in each case probably due to language misunderstanding. The white man was being paid 2 and a half times the rate paid to an African or Chinese for similar if not identical work. This was pursuant to rates agreed between the Government and white unions.

As an athlete and sportsman himself, George ensured that ERPM had the best sports ground along the reef together with an adjoining cricket pitch but whether these facilities were open to all races is not clear.

Muriel

CHAPTER 8

As far as one can gauge the children were all fond of their father but they did not see a great deal of him. They had a series of governesses and nannies and the eldest Helen, Muriel and Gwen were all dressed alike and did everything together. Muriel said that they did not feel like other individual children. There was a touching note to Gwen when she won a gymkhana in Johannesburg and was complimented on her riding skills. George was very fond of sending telegrams and whenever the girls were taking exams, he would send them a telegram which read 'Best wishes for today'. That was probably heart felt as he had not been particularly good at exams himself. When each of the eldest four were studying abroad he would impress upon them the importance of learning all they could about the conditions of the country. They all felt they had disappointed their parents because they were not boys. One cannot help wondering how that must have affected their psychological makeup.

At the Pretoria Eisteddford in May 2007 according to The Rand Daily Mail, Muriel ('little Miss Farrar') sang with great feeling, pure enunciation and a well-trained voice. In the Cello solo Miss Gwendoline Farrar ran away from all the other competitors and was adjudged an easy first. With Gwendoline Farrar one must not say 'prodigy' at her age but particularly in her encore she displayed a touch and tone which is clearly exceptional in the lovely Berceuse she chose. In a scene from 'Alice in Wonderland all 4 (the quartet now included 7 year old Marjorie) are to be commended on their skill as musicians. In the gymkhana which followed Miss Muriel Farrar in all paces was a good second but unlike the rider her mount lacked polish'.

Ella also organised concerts at Chicheley at which all 4 performed. George himself was not at all musical but he enjoyed listening to the

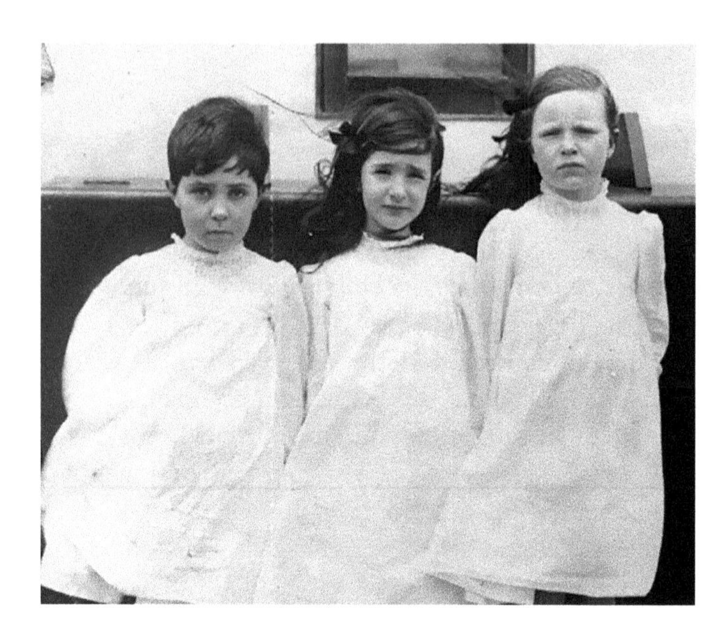

Gwendoline, Muriel and Helen

Gwen, aged 16 years

children playing, above all Gwen, and he loved hearing Ella sing especially when she sang 'When swallows homeward fly', particularly appropriate since perforce she spent such long periods away. Muriel wrote to George about her Granny, George's mother, a little differently to how she records her in her memoir: 'She gets up every morning for breakfast at 9 and then does the housekeeping and then goes shopping. After that she comes home to lunch and reads the news and is upstairs in the afternoon and does not go to bed till 10. She is quite extraordinary'.

George writing to Helen on the same subject: 'Granny is a very clever and wise old lady and you can learn much from her, as I always do. People who have lived a number of years as she has, get vast experience and knowledge only obtainable through a life of practical experience. One can read a great deal in books but real practical experience is the best schoolmaster of all'.

Muriel was sent off to a pension in Germany when she was just 16 and there are several warm letters from her father. Sadly, she does

Back row: Helen and Muriel.
In front: Marjorie, Ella, baby Ella, Kate and Gwen.
Below: a boy guest, possibly the son of one of the servants

not refer to this period in her memoir but it must have been incredibly difficult for her. When she became engaged her mother Ella, went off to help her choose items for their first house. Neither George nor Ella would have appreciated the fact that after they had produced 4 girls the chances of a boy turning up the odds would have crept up to something like 250 to one against and after 5 the odds would have grown to something like 1,000 to one and had they known my mother would in all probability never have been born nor me.

Ella was by nature gregarious and loved entertaining at Bedford with numerous garden parties. I cannot date either of these incidents. The first is c.1903. George returns home late on a Friday. Without informing George, Ella has arranged that they will accompany their neighbours in their old-fashioned caravan to the *bundu*, with 2 African servants. George will bring his shotgun in order to shoot their dinner, which their African cook will braivleis for them. George duly finds and shoots a brace of partridges. Afterwards the bridge table is brought out and they play bridge by candlelight.

The second incident was planned for months. It was a visit to The Victoria Falls, which Ella describes in 55 pages in a bound volume. The volume is undated but the trip occurred in about April 1907. My aunt Kate then known as Kathleen had been born in 1906. I think Ella enjoyed the fact that people begged her not to go. George clearly knew better than to make any attempt to dissuade her. George placed a severe limit on the amount of luggage they could take (Ella had to reduce 5 large suitcases to 1) because, although the trip to Bulawayo was a relatively straight forward and indeed a comfortable train journey on a night train via Bloemfontein and Mafeking, when they reached the railhead beyond M'Banji there remained a 130 mile trek across undeveloped, what Ella describes as 'lion' country, which she was to negotiate by waggon while George and Col. Franky Rhodes, who accompanied them from there, went on horseback. The waggon was extremely uncomfortable for her; the wheels frequently hit stumps of trees. Eventually Ella got them to unharness one of the mules drawing the waggon, which she then rode which was more comfortable. Ella changed to a pony, which she rode alternately astride and then straddle (side saddle) to prevent the pony getting a sore back. They travelled about 17 miles a day. They heard the roar before they could actually see what the natives called 'the smoke', the dense vapour that hovers above the Falls. Ella examined The Falls from every possible angle and took some amazing photographs and detailed notes. She visited Livingstone Island paddled by one African. Dr Livingstone had planted trees there but unfortunately they had been eaten by hippopotami. She crossed The Devil's Gulley on a zipwire. On the return journey they stayed at Government House in Bulawayo, and Ella sat under a tree where Lobengula used to hold court every morning and she imagined him pronouncing sentence of 'immediate elimination' upon members of the opposition in his Council. George gave a condensed version of the trip at the Community centre in Boksburg on the 6th November 2007.

Ella decided on a bizarre occasion at which to launch her youngest child (my mother, also called Ella) into the entertainment business. For some reason the New Zealand navy were moored at Durban just 4 months prior to the First world war being declared and a selection made their way to Johannesburg and they were invited to one of Ella's garden parties at Bedford Farm. She commissioned my mother then aged just 3 to carry a tray bearing pipes and tobacco and to present it to each of the sailors with instructions to perform the ceremony carefully. She selected first the tallest person she could see who happened to be the gaunt figure of the Bishop of Pretoria, who stooped low to secure his prize. In addition to garden parties the Johannesburg telephone messenger boys were allowed to have picnics at Bedford on selected days.

Ella crossing Devils Gulley adjoining the Victoria Falls

CHAPTER 9

For so long as George was able to give his full attention ERPM thrived. All mines were forced to close for the duration of the war from 1899-1902. When war broke out in 1899 some 12,000 non- Boers fled from the mining areas of the Transvaal to Natal and Cape Province. George joined his brother Percy in forming The Kaffrarian Rifles. Some were local residents in Natal but a substantial number were drawn from those who had fled. It is not clear how much consent was given by shareholders but EPRM appears to have underwritten the cost of forming the regiment. Percy and George held commissions as Captain; George was later appointed a major on the staff of the Colonial Division. He proved to be 'one of General Brabant's most trusted and reliable Intelligence officers throughout The Orange Free State and Transvaal campaigns.'

His secretary, H. Webber, notes an incident before war broke out which 'illustrates vividly his complete fearlessness which gave him ascendancy over other men. He went to Fordsburg. It had been announced in advance that he would speak from a waggon at the corner of the square. The audience was very hostile. He began his speech: 'What made me keen on coming to speak to you chaps tonight was that I got several messages to say if I came, I'd be shot. Here I am. Now who has the pluck to shoot me?' Scowls of hate and threats turned to cheers.

Rhodes was convinced that Kruger would never fight over the issue of the right to be treated as a citizen; Chamberlain issued an ultimatum to the Transvaal Government to enter negotiations to determine the rights of those living in the Transvaal to be treated as citizens. Although Kruger had a profound belief that emancipation was a matter for him to determine he expressed a willingness to negotiate. Hofmeyr was accepted by both sides as a mediator. His recommendations were ignored by the High Commissioner and

George in military Kaffrarian uniforms

22. 1. 1900.

The bearer, Mr. George Farrar, has full authority to organize the recruiting, the equipping and purchase of horses in the Cape Colony for Brigadier General Brabant's Colonial Division, and to proceed by rail or Steamer to any part of the Cape Colony.
The Military and Railway Authorities will please give him every assistance to facilitate this object.

Kitchener

Authority from Kitchener organising recruiting, equipping and purchase of horses during the Boer war

by Chamberlain. Despite strong opposition from the Liberal Opposition in Whitehall, Chamberlain's ultimatum was approved by Parliament. Upon learning that troops had been moved up to the Transvaal borders, Kruger declared that there would have to be war; he felt the need to strike the first blow before the British could deploy their full strength.

Pretoria maintained that under the 1894 Act Transvaal was to be treated as a sovereign state. In the House of Commons Lord Derby maintained that if you examined the preamble to the Act the United Kingdom was the sovereign state and that a sovereign state cannot be expected to settle disputes with her vassal state by arbitration.

The Standard and Diggers' News was a very large journal printed mainly in English with a mass of advertisements in wide circulation throughout the mines. Its leaders were consistently supportive of the Government and The Het Volk policy, but on some occasions their views were dispassionate and carefully reasoned but often racial as in 'The native menace'. Here is a selection of their leaders leading up to and immediately following Kruger's declaration of war:

'The fact that Mr. Hofmeyr is again brought into a deputation to Pretoria in the interests of peace is its own criticism upon the diplomacy of Chamberlain and Sir A. Milner (High Commissioner and soon to become Lord Milner), whose failure is proclaimed at every point of the compass by the presence of troops in the country and the fact that burghers are massed on the border. Their presence means that diplomats have failed to get a grip of the situation and that they find themselves in need of local help. Chamberlain and Milner are lacking in imagination. Chamberlain is a hard and fast businessman. Milner is a master of figures and a mathematician. They both fail on statesmanship.

The present situation is due to the policy of the Pushful. When Chamberlain came to power and started his career as an Empire builder, he had a fixed idea that the world was there to be dragooned into his way of thinking, that distant lands and peoples could be controlled on the principle of the counting house and that sentiments were of no account. A great Empire is a fine thing to dream about. Though he may have had imagination to build a castle in the air he does not understand that an Empire built on force and mere discipline rests upon an indifferent and dangerous basis and that no grand or permanent results have been achieved in that way, by mere edicts inspired by an iron will. History ought to have taught him that. The statesman makes himself certain of all the facts, notes the feelings, has regards for the sentiments even though they may be far removed from those in Whitehall and steers his way carefully among them conceding here and there, conciliating all the time. There has been no conciliation here, an essential for the man who seeks to rule. South Africa had been working out its own salvation shaping its own destiny and going along quietly and prosperously. When Chamberlain appeared and applied his pace quickening methods, South Africa should have been the last country to which the Imperial accelerando was applied. A man of imagination would have seen where this rough riding principle was bound to lead but Chamberlain had no imagination only his fixed idea of imperial might, headed and or supported by Rhodes. Kruger said there must be war but Chamberlain provoked him.

George thought Chamberlain was a bully and felt that he treated South Africa like a spoilt child but he respected Milner and after the war, when Milner displayed considerable statesmanship, developed a close relationship with him. Hofmeyr was under instructions to accept a 5 year residency before the right to vote but it does not appear that Kruger was ever prepared to offer anything other than 15 years.

'For many months we have preached peace and forbearance. We set out what war would mean for Johannesburg. We predicted vividly enough the ruin it would bring upon thousands of our population. It is only now that the population is discovering how correct we were. The labour of years is gone and we face ruin. All that is left now is Mr. Rhodes' cheque book to assist people out of Johannesburg to stays elsewhere'.

A particularly poignant and pungent letter to the editor caught my eye and reads:

'Putting aside all sentiment and humbug about Uitlanders' hardships there is no just cause for war to be made on Transvaal by Great Britain. Everyone agrees that the form of Government of the Transvaal could be improved upon, that Kruger and his counsellors would be well advised to make their franchise laws less strict and did away with some of the taxes but every sensible man in South Africa must also allow that these disabilities and restrictions ... are far too slight to justify the shedding of innocent blood. Workers for large railway and dock companies disaffected by their wages or hours sometimes strike to get their grievances redressed but what would be said if they murdered the relatives and children of the directors in order to obtain the concessions they sought'.

On the 5th October 1999 the Government approved the confiscation of property, entering mines and removing gold and commandeering any gold found in transit.

After 10 days of war: 'A peaceful and flourishing country has been converted into a battlefield; peaceful vocations have been replaced by a call to arms. The home of commerce has given way to the roar of cannons. Bridges have fallen and railways been destroyed'. The siege of Mafeking was an early success for the Boers. Lucas Meyer, now a General impresses the opposing troops. Dr Coster, the State Prosecutor is one of the many left dead after the battle of Elandslaagte. Also now promoted to General is the Capt. White, who possessed the incriminating documents in The Jameson raid. He speaks about the performance of the enemy at Elandslaagte. There are encouraging accounts of how ambulance crews worked together after the battle of Ladysmith and the Boer press spoke of the courtesy and kindness shown. No atrocities were committed before the arrival of Kitchener but I am drawing a veil over what happened then. There was a scorched earth policy with which we are all too familiar, needless destruction of farmsteads and herding of people into camps. There were 8,000 Britons in action before the arrival of troops from Australia and New Zealand, after which the Boers were heavily outnumbered.

There were strong calls for peace from the Church, the Liberal party in The House of Commons and other countries led by France.

George took part in operations in the Transvaal and in The Orange Free State including the relief of Wepener, which lies on the eastern edge of Basutoland, where his brother Percy had been besieged. The siege was lifted on April 22nd and thereafter on that day George always sent a telegram to all old comrades, especially Percy. He was promoted to Major. George was mentioned in dispatches in 1901, received the Queen's medal with 4 clasps and was awarded the DSO in April 2001 and was knighted in 1902 in recognition of his services during hostilities. Percy, who had been seriously wounded in August 2000, also received the Queen's medal and the DSO. On the 12th May a deputation containing President Steyn (Orange Free State) who had wanted to continue fighting, and deputy President Schalk Burger (Transvaal) and Generals Louis Botha, Jan Smuts (Transvaal) and Christiaan de Wet and Koos de la Rey (Orange Free State) was detailed to hand over to Kitchener a draft Treaty of friendship seeking pre-war status, but with votes for Uitlanders and a commercial union with GB. English and Dutch to be recognised as official languages and a general amnesty. Kitchener was astounded. He sent the proposal to London with recommendation that discussions should continue. Milner was very hostile demanding unconditional surrender and insisting on free rein for the administration of both Boer republics as colonies of the Crown.

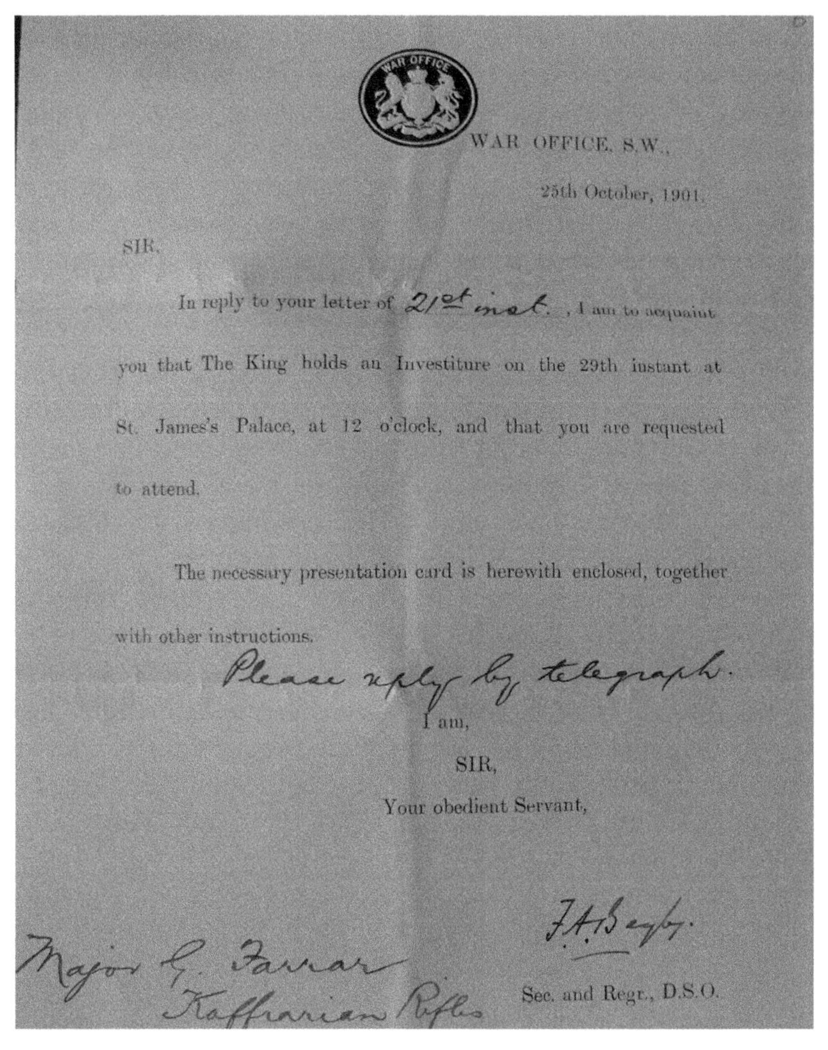

WAR OFFICE

WAR OFFICE, S.W.,

25th October, 1901.

SIR,

In reply to your letter of 21st inst., I am to acquaint you that The King holds an Investiture on the 29th instant at St. James's Palace, at 12 o'clock, and that you are requested to attend.

The necessary presentation card is herewith enclosed, together with other instructions.

Please reply by telegraph.

I am,

SIR,

Your obedient Servant,

F.A. Bagby.

Sec. and Regr., D.S.O.

Major G. Farrar
Kaffrarian Rifles

George received the Queen's medal with
4 clasps and DSO in 1901

Three days later 30 representatives from the Orange Free State and the Transvaal met at Vereeniging to see whether they could agree a revised proposal to negotiate the terms of a surrender. After a heated debate Louis Botha proposed including a request for £3 million for war reparations, to be paid by the British. Because the Orange Free State wished to continue fighting this would be confined to Transvaal. On the British side Chamberlain had been arguing for some time that any agreement must include black emancipation. To counter this Smuts provided a clause that this should be suspended until self-government for the Transvaal was realised. The British accepted this proposal 'in the interests of reaching agreement', thereby setting a precedent for what occurred 7 years later at the formation of The Union. Having initially only offered £1 million they did agree to pay Louis Botha's request for £3 million for war damage reparation. Although it is described as The Peace of Vereeniging it was signed in Melrose House, Pretoria.

In 1903 George was elected President of the Witwatersrand Chamber of Mines and when responsible government returned to Transvaal, he was unanimously elected leader of the Progressive Party which effectively meant that he was Leader of the Opposition to the Ministry of General Louis Botha. His constituency was Boksburg and his opponent was Walter Madeley, who was one of his employees, who had supported Kruger and disliked rule from Whitehall. Kruger supported the wide differential in pay for white employees, which George thought to be unjustified. George stipulated a date when he reserved the conference hall at ERPM and his opponent and employee was permitted to have the hall on any other date of their choice. Helen, Muriel and Gwen campaigned on their ponies with a placard saying 'Vote for Daddy'. George was elected by 716 votes to 398.

George as parliamentarian and Leader of the opposition

CHAPTER 10

Initially George was a hesitant speaker but he gradually gained confidence mastering his subject and growing in authority. There was difficulty in recruiting enough Africans to go underground because witch doctors were advising them that it was dangerous. How right they were! The vast majority of those willing to work underground came from Portuguese colonies. There were very few from South Africa or the Protectorates. George wanted to recruit Chinese workers and at one point Italian workers and to import them. This policy was not popular initially even among mine owners. Afrikaners and Africans were opposed albeit for slightly different reasons. The loudest objectors were Boers but they were joined by English members of the white Miners Union. It was based on a heady cocktail of xenophobia coupled with a fear of loss of some jobs and a weakening of wage negotiating position and they enjoyed strong support from the Verkramptes wing of The Nationalist governing party. George made a speech lasting 3 hours and mustering a majority, around to his view. As part of his argument, he said that the builders of The Panama Canal imported Chinese labour having discovered that white labour was ill suited to the task. The Johannesburg Times reported: 'He put his case in logical clear headed fashion showing at all times his ready wit and quick gift of repartee; even his opponents admitted what a fair fighter he was especially when he had his back to the wall. It then fell to him as leader of the unofficial members in the legislative Council to bring forward the detailed bill setting out all the necessary amendments to existing law, which he did in a speech lasting 5 hours so that Chinese labour was then introduced into the mines. It was not an unqualified success because of language difficulties leading to misunderstandings. The reaction in London was reported thus: 'From the beginning Her Majesty's Government regarded the import of Chinese labour as an experiment and was accepted by the Liberal Government as necessary to meet a serious shortage of labour. It was permitted as a supplement to and not as a substitute for Kaffir labour. By 1958 the word 'Kaffir' was derogatory and offensive although still in common use. In fact, the word does not appear to have any African origins, save that there is a Kaffir River in the Orange Free State. Its original meaning was an inhabitant of Kaffriristan, which was a part of India. After it fell out of common use it continued to be used in reference to South African mining shares on the Stock Exchange.

The Progressives felt that they had won the argument for Chinese labour in Parliament but the strength of feeling outside Parliament never really abated. On the 23rd August 2006 the Rand Daily Mail reported on an outdoor meeting in Fordsburg: 'To anyone acquainted with the feeling in Fordsburg it must have seemed foolhardy on the part of the Progressives to hold an open meeting in a district where the odds against them obtaining a fair hearing were lowly indeed. It speaks volumes for the pluck and determination of the Progressives that they disclaimed to resort to a ticket meeting packed with their own supporters but took the risk of appealing to the spirit of fair play'. But it was typical George. 'Sir George was by no means disconcerted by this decidedly unflattering reception. He was coolness personified and a smile played over his features as he calmly surveyed the howling mob. Shouts were raised that the meeting should adjourn to Market Square. Sir George expressed his willingness to go anywhere and the entire crowd trooped off to Market Square'.

'An impromptu platform was formed using an auctioneers' rostrum and chairs were provided for speakers and some members of the Press who were enterprising enough to clamber up on to the somewhat perilous platform and the opposition surrounded them. The crowd by this time had increased to very large dimensions. There were several uncommitted people anxious to hear Sir George, who maintained his *sang froid* saying he would state his views and then take any questions. Despite countless interruptions he made himself heard. One individual kept on at him. Sir George said he thought he should come on to the platform with him so that he could be better heard and gave him a hand up'. It was a tactic he would employ to good effect on other occasions on the hustings.

In Parliament George had announced the policy of the Progressives to be: 'that the state must favour neither the miner nor the cultivators of land nor the merchants nor the manufacturers but a balance of the whole'.

There was a strong vote of confidence in George's nomination at a meeting at Benoni on the 24th January 1907 when the motion for him to stand was carried by 550 votes to 9 against.

The Transvaal leader on the 1st February reads: 'As far as electors are concerned it is natural that they should interest themselves chiefly in those matters which most nearly concern them. It is a common law of psychology that human interest in any event depends largely on details of a local character rather than upon Imperial issues. A superficial glance at the questions to candidates at any particular meeting makes this quite clear. The bulk of the questions are confined to a very narrow and circumscribed area. There is a danger of mistaking the cackle of the bourg for a factor of national importance. The fight which Sir Percy (Fitzgerald) is making in Pretoria is one which centre's the attention of all politicians who think imperially, and his victory would mean a triumph of broad over narrow minds and a defeat of that monstrous dream of South Africa as an amputated and bleeding limb of Empire ... Similarly, whether Sir George Farrar wins his seat at Boksburg is a matter on which great issues turn. This conflict will determine whether the people of Boksburg are prepared to jeopardise an industry on which the town and country depend, or that they are determined to support an industrial enterprise and the freedom of South Africa to control its own domestic policy. The spectacle of a working man opposing his employer in a conflict for political honours must be extremely rare. None know better than miners themselves the treatment they have received at the hands of the owners and the conditions under which their work is done, and no section of the community is better acquainted with the need for unskilled coloured labour for the prosperity of the gold industry. When the miners of the East Rand return Sir George Farrar at the head of the Poll it is an expression of the utmost confidence in him as a capitalist, faith in the principles for which he stands as the leader of the Progressive cause and a vindication of indentured coloured labour in spite of the fierce antagonism of the forces of prejudice, ignorance and misrepresentation.'

Even up to the eve of the election in 1907 the Progressives under George were bullish about actually winning the election. Reporting on a meeting held at The Wanderers Club on the 15th February 1907: 'They (The Progressives) have been through the fire of ceaseless calumny and vile misrepresentation. It has been exposed to hostility, indecent but unconcealed by the ascendant political party in Great Britain. Sir George Farrar has never acquitted himself better on any platform. His speech was concise, statesmanlike and rousing. Under his leadership the Progressive army goes in to battle strong, united and confident of victory'. In the event the Progressives were crushed; only Percy Fitzpatrick was a surprise winner in Pretoria and George retained his seat comfortably. The Rand Daily Mail reported: 'In the return of Sir George Farrar by a crushing majority the workmen of the East Rand have declared their undiminished faith in the principles of the Progressive cause and silenced forever the anti-capitalist cry as hollow. Few men like Sir George have been made the shafts of abuse and slander because coincidentally with their possession of wealth they were enthused with a genuine patriotism, which found expression in the most disinterested efforts for the wealth of this country. It is not too much to say that the indebtedness of the East Rand to Sir George Farrar cannot be overestimated and taking a still wider view it is not too much to say that his work and worth will be permanently associated with all that is best in the development and progress of South Africa. He has been opposed in the present campaign by a Labour candidate who is one of his own employees, a fact which speaks volumes concerning the freedom of political action in the Transvaal and furnishes a crushing answer to the pernicious false accusation of the Radicals that the workmen of the Rand were oppressed by an iron heel'. The Star, which was a pro Progressive tabloid reporting on the 16th April 1907: 'It is clear that the Opposition is in no way dismayed by their crushing defeat. Sir George does not reproach the British who deserted their kindred in droves and played into the hands of the party with whom politically they have nothing in common. He ascribed it to their ignorance of the political history of The Transvaal'. The Progressives pointed to the successes of Canada and Australia. They wanted to see similar enterprise and prosperity in South Africa. George criticized the followers of Hertzog: 'The old school want to be left alone. They are still voortrekkers at heart. They suspect any new ideas. They regard Smuts and Botha as being, too British, too hasty and too advanced. Like Kruger they fear being drowned by the British'. George felt that the Opposition should shift the battleground to support the Government in all areas where backwoodsmen could be exposed.

In 1907 Johannesburg celebrated its 21st birthday and the Rand Daily Mail produced a celebratory edition from which I have selected a few snippets: 'In 20 years it has grown from a bare stretch of veldt to become the largest city in South Africa, which would not disgrace central London today. The Rand is now the largest gold producer in the world. If a country is in the happy position of having no history the next best thing is to be able to forget history quickly. The Transvaal has suffered from an oversupply of history and the only consolation is for it to be able to forget history quickly.

'In few lands do memories of the past fade so rapidly. A stranger from England seeing The House of Assembly in action in Pretoria for the first time and not having read about events of the past decade, would be struck by the spectacle of Sir George Farrar discussing the detail of Mr. Gregorowski's Law Agent's Bill. For 10 years ago, Mr. then Judge Gregorowski had sentenced Sir George to death. He could not hear The Prime Minister or General Smuts without remembering that only 5 years ago they had signed The Peace of Vereeniging. But happily the Transvaal does not worry about these things.

'In this respect one can honestly pay tribute to both Briton and Boer. The first session of the Transvaal's first responsible Parliament is over. And it has been absolutely free of rancour. In the main the Transvaal has forgotten the bloody battles of the past. For this at least Providence can be thanked. The losers have won. And they have forgotten they ever lost. Which is perhaps the best ending of all. Caution has been the keynote of The Government's policy.

Caution was an equally marked characteristic of The Opposition. Political division is mainly racial but I very much doubt whether there will not be big changes. No doubt the Boers will have a majority in The Cape as well as The Orange Free State and the Transvaal but the Dutch phalanx in the Transvaal is not as solid as it looks. The Dutch leaders have difficulty in controlling their followers. Botha, Smuts and de Villiers are progressive in temperament but their followers are not'.

The Progressives' policies and tactics appear to have been largely devised by George. He gave full support to The Prime Minister on his upcoming visit to London urging him to stop Whitehall treating South Africa like a spoilt child and respect its adulthood. He fully supported General Smuts plans for education and urged him to make school attendance compulsory.

On the 26th June 1905 the largest ever diamond was found at the Premier no. 2 mine near Kimberley and was named after the owner of the mine, Thomas Cullinan. Weighing in at 3,106.75 carats it was more than three times the previous largest, found at Jagersfontein just 80 miles south of Kimberley in 1893. Nothing comparable has been found since. It went on display at the Standard Bank in Johannesburg and was seen by 8,500 people. It was then sent to Premier's London agents. Due to its immense value detectives were assigned to the steamboat rumoured to be carrying it and it was ceremoniously locked in the captain's safe and guarded for the entire journey but this was a ruse. The stone on the boat was a fake. The real stone was sent in a plain box via registered post! Despite considerable interest it remained unsold by L. Neumann for 2 years. In the face of this setback Thomas Cullinan decided that he would like to present it as a gift to The King, Edward V11. He could have done so himself or on behalf of Griqualand West, which may still have been a separate British Crown Colony, which following numerous claims by other parties, it had become in August 1873.However as mentioned earlier a dubious piece of legislation called The Griqualand Annexation Act passed on 27th July 1877 purported to end Griqualand's independence and Griqualand West would appear to have accepted that situation despite retaining its own Supreme Court.

Quite why Thomas Cullinan approached Louis Botha for his advice is not entirely clear but in August 2007 the Prime Minister acting on behalf of the Transvaal had purchased the diamond from Thomas Cullinan for the sum of £150,000 (£16 million in 2019) provisionally, on condition that the Legislative Council approve his intention to present it the King 'as a token of the loyalty and attachment of the people of Transvaal to His Majesty's throne and person'. To the surprise of some and the fury of Louis Botha and Jan Smuts, George voted against the proposal. He felt that it was an inappropriate gesture at a time when the economy was only just beginning to recover. It would be better to place the diamond back on display in Johannesburg to encourage foreign visitors. The motion was nevertheless carried by 42 votes to 19. Initially the British Prime Minister Henry Campbell Bannerman advised the King against accepting the gift but later left the choice to The King. He was finally persuaded by Winston Churchill to accept. The diamond was then sent to J.L. Asscher in Amsterdam to be cut. After weeks of planning it then took 8 months with 3 people working 14 hours a day to complete the task. Making the first incision was extremely difficult and risky. At the first attempt the steel knife broke but the second knife inserted in a small groove split it into two pieces. It was cut in to 105 separate stones the largest of which is Cullinan 1 or 'The Star of Africa' and is moulded into The Royal Sceptre. At 530.4 carats it is the largest clear-cut diamond in the world. Cullinan 2 is mounted into The Imperial State Crown and is the second largest clear-cut diamond in the world. There were 9 major stones. All but the first 2 major stones remained in Amsterdam by arrangement as fee for Asscher's services until The South African Government bought them except for Cullinan VI, which Edward bought for his Queen Alexandra. The High Commissioner later presented 2 to Queen Mary, one to Louis Botha, one to the diamond merchants who supervised the cutting and one to Jacob Romijn, who founded the first Trade Union in the diamond industry, which would appear to leave 2 unaccounted for. When George and Louis Botha were asked to lunch at Buckingham Palace the diamonds were on display. I think George must have squirmed a little when the Queen leant over to LB and said, 'I believe we have you to thank for this extraordinary gift'. What was surely most remarkable was that just 5 years prior to his proposal to the Legislative Council Louis Botha had been at war with the British.

In early 2008 The Government voted to end the giving of licenses to registered Chinese labour. This followed a concerted campaign by The Prime Minister and General Smuts in particular, the Liberal Party in Whitehall, and the white trade unions, but it was a sad day for the Chinese and for George who had invested so much in them and been lambasted for doing so. Remarkable statements were made in parliament. The Prime Minister stated that if Chinese labour remained in the country there could be no prosperity for whites. Smuts echoed this sentiment calling them 'The yellow peril' and went on to state that during strikes they continued working; some mines continued working almost without white labour. It probably does not say much for working conditions in China at the time, but the Chinese were grateful for the work and to express their gratitude to the Mine Managers they staged each Christmas Chinese pantomimes for the children at the mine. In 2007 at the Rose Deep mine in Germiston 2000 Chinese held a thanksgiving ceremony for the Manager of the mine.

Our 'Native' Labour Supply.
Smuts kicking the Chinese out of the labour force

George was also a member of the Inter Colonial Council whose chief work was regulation of the Railways, an issue about which he had been so critical in the early days. One of his political adversaries, a man called Hay made a speech in a public meeting held in the Presbyterian church in Braamfontein in which he said: 'We have heard of the iniquity of concessions and monopolies under Krugerism. Well, we have had an oligarchy of a different kind since the war. We have had Sir George Farrar as head of The Railway Committee charged with great public trust and what do we find? We find he sat there as Chairman and allowed concessions to be given to his friends and associates for construction of the Witbank Springs line'. George issued proceedings for slander. It was contended that by those words Hay had implied that George had been guilty of dishonesty, corruption and breach of trust in the discharge of his duty as Chairman of The Railway Committee and was not a fit and proper person to occupy that position and had been greatly injured in his good name and claimed damages in the sum of £5,000. The matter came on before Rose Innes LJ, the same man who had

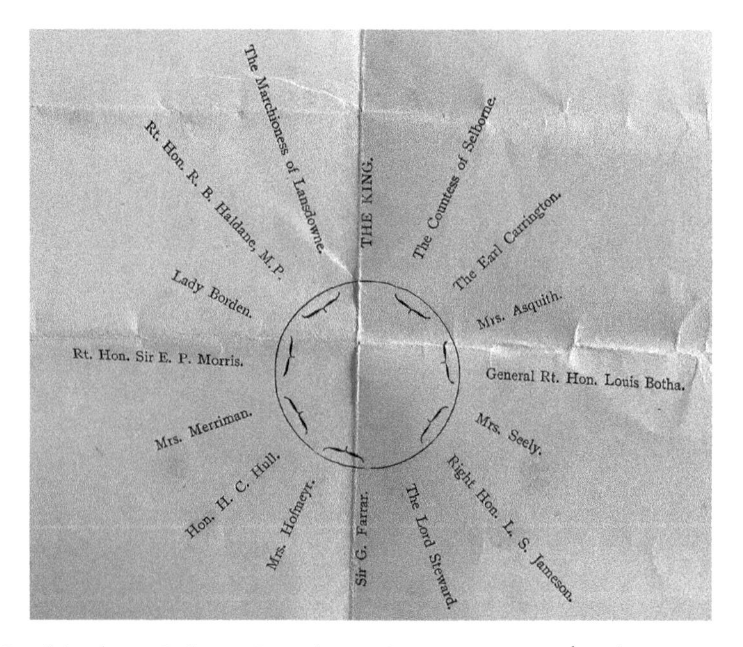

Buckingham Palace. Luncheon Sitting List. 24th July 1909.
Sir George Farrar's table

Lady Farrar's table

originally been briefed to defend George and the other members of The Reform Committee, but who had been elevated to Lord Chief Justice in the interim, now presiding in The Supreme Court in Pretoria. In fact George was not Chairman but simply a member of the Board. He had taken particular steps to make sure he had nothing to do with the case on account of his association and had been in England at the time the case was being heard. Mr Hay's counsel ran some improbable defences. Words were not accurate. Reporter with shorthand training rebutted that. Words were not false, scandalous or malicious or defamatory. Even if they *were* used, they were a fair comment, none of which found favour with the court and Mr. Hay would have had a much more expensive day in court had George not made an unfortunate remark when being examined in chief by his own counsel: 'Do you consider yourself damaged by this'? (The offending statement) 'Unless I clear myself it is impossible for me to continue in public life'. Under cross examination: 'Since the statement was made you have been elected to Parliament and made leader of the Opposition'. George won the case with costs and was awarded £1,000 in damages.

ERPM was now registered in London and had an office in Fenchurch St. Sidney who had left South Africa some years before, oversaw the London office. This is taken from a London Stock Market report: 'George Farrar, now 42 looks younger. He is an active restless man with small, deep-set eyes, a firm closely set mouth and chin, which reveals the dogged tenacity of his nature. Some say he is cold, hard and even unsympathetic. Others will tell you he is a generous warm-hearted man whose coldness is only skin deep. My impression is that he is both. When he came to seek his fortune he was just 19, a bracing youth with pluck, shrewdness, a capacity for slogging work and a determination to locate for himself a lasting position.'

George began his speech by explaining why this was an extraordinary meeting and could not be held on a regular basis. 'A meeting here involves considerable practical difficulties and considerable expense. A journey of 14,000 miles and 2 months absence for one of the directors and 2 months absence from the headquarters of the company but there are now a large number of shareholders here and I am here to answer any of your questions.

'I have to smile even in this grave contingency when I reflect that this concern employs some 17,000 people, produces one tenth of the gold of the entire Witwatersrand, the greatest and most consistent gold producing centre of the civilised world. There is probably no industrial concern in this country and few in the United States which for elaborate organisation, for intricacy of scientific treatment and for general success can compare with the company at the head of which I have stood since its inception 18 years ago.' These were the desperate and bold words of a man under pressure. He spoke of the company's substantial reserves, how UK companies enjoyed more generous allowances for depreciation of Plant and committed himself to reducing costs.

The Investors Chronicle reporting on the meeting: 'Sir George Farrar has faced the music and may be said to have survived the ordeal well. The tussle between him and the Central Mining Group has

Very Elementary Education
George explaining to shareholders why ERPM profits have gone down

resulted in the expected compromises. Sir George thinks costs can be brought down'.

A shareholder wrote in: 'I was greatly impressed with Farrar. He was a man I'd never seen. I went to the meeting feeling critical and censorious but I came away most favourably impressed owing to Sir George's straightforward manly behaviour and I think the majority of unbiassed people felt the same way as I did at the end of the meeting.'

As the leader of the Opposition George was one of the delegates to the National Convention from which the foundation stones of The Union of South Africa were laid. He believed in the ideal and worked strenuously for it. George was opposed to a federation because he believed it to be 'entirely unsuited to the needs of South Africa. They must build anew and avoid the blunders of the past.

To the people of Natal some of whom appear to regard Union with fear and anxiety I say: Trust the people of Transvaal. There the British and the Boer have been brought together by the wise and tolerant words of General Botha and General Smuts and they stand together inviting you to join a union of the whole of South Africa. Speaking for myself and those whose views I know I represent, I declare that we have total faith in the sincerity of General Botha and General Smuts'. He appears to have struck a lasting rapport with Louis Botha who trusted him.

On the 4th February 1909 he made an important speech which began: 'Remember whatever sacrifices are made they are but temporary as the only road to lasting peace and prosperity is through union. On the other hand, who can tell the price that may be paid through disunion.' It ended with these words: 'If South Africa is to fulfil its destiny unhampered by internal strife and discussion it must have a sovereign Parliament and a Government delegating the powers of a local parliament. I agree with those who regard the native problem in South Africa as one which demands the utmost care and most delicate handling and one which demands a united response. If we fail, I fear we will drift into civil war again'.

This came after George had given a press release after the Convention: 'The Transvaal Progressives believe in proportional representation which would greatly reduce the racial element from politics by giving each section of the population an opportunity of obtaining fair representation particularly in the case of minorities in country districts'. Quite what this would have entailed in practice for native Africans is not clear. It may simply have raised the position of Africans to that of Cape Coloureds in the Cape Colony. They had an agreed number of seats in the Cape Colony Parliament and emancipation was limited to the rateable value of households. It was originally £25 but Cecil Rhodes effectively reduced emancipation by increasing the required value of a household from £25 to £75. George went on to explain that: it was hopeless to get sufficient support for it in the Convention ... they met the attack on it by demanding that the part of the constitution embodying the principle of equal representation as between town and country should be especially safeguarded against the possibility of attack in the Union Parliament'. The Convention met them by offering them an appeal to the Imperial Government on any question effecting the representation of the people in The House of Assembly. The issue of racial inequality, which had clearly been raised and was arguably within the original Constitution was then totally ignored. Once the Unionist party, which largely absorbed the Progressives was formed, the issue was not raised again in the national parliament until the late 1950s when the new Progressive party was formed. By then The Unionist party had fully accepted the principle of apartheid with its accompanying denial of human rights. This denial was rationalised by a deeply held belief that the African belonged to an inferior race; this belief was by no means confined to Boers but it was supported by The Dutch Reformed Church. Another analogous irrational belief was that skilled jobs needed to be the sole preserve of white people *in order to protect poor whites* from the apparently inferior race.

A remarkable tribute to the leading personalities of the Convention was paid in the House of Commons by Colonel Seely, the Under Secretary of State for the Colonies: 'The greatest credit will be accorded to those men English and Dutch, who after waging a terrible war set their minds to work to heal animosities, to such men as those who met at Durban and Cape town and have set the whole world a splendid example of what could be done in healing racial feuds to such men as General Botha and ex-President Steyn on the one hand and Sir George Farrar and Doctor Jameson on the other, who lead their people from so desperate a conflict to so great a reconciliation.' The late Lord De Villiers, the President of The Convention also paid tribute to George when speaking at Paarl in 2007: 'You may not have agreed with his policy in the past (I think a reference to Chinese labour) but you may take it from me that the interests of South Africa as a whole were as dear to him as to any other delegate at the Convention and that The Cape will gain and not lose by entering into partnership with another Colony, which provides men of his calibre.'

In the subsequent election George had a strenuous fight in Georgetown (Transvaal) winning by 1104 votes against H.C. Hall, who later became Finance Minister and Tom Matthews the miners' leader, who George thought was a communist. In this election Ella frequently addressed meetings of electors filling in for George.

EPRM suffered when George was devoting all his energies to politics and in 1911, the year of my mother's birth, he left the Assembly and quit politics having given his pledge to shareholders to do so at the at the previous AGM. In the New Year's Honours List of 1911, he was made a baronet for his contribution to the formation of The Union.

Leaving the Foreign Office with Botha having presented their petition for the Union of S. Africa

CHAPTER 11

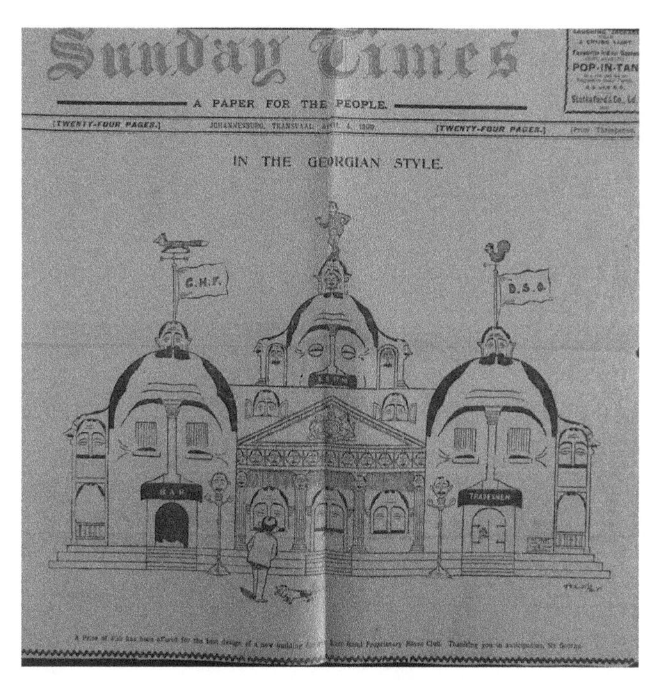

In the Georgian Style
A Prize of £25 has been offered for the best design of
a new building for the East Rand proprietary Mines Club

The pressure to increase production and to reduce costs is one faced by all mining companies but as the cartoons illustrate, the inspiration and management of the entire enterprise of ERPM was the brainchild of one man. While George was fighting a war, away for long periods in Parliament or fighting an election, things did not run smoothly and other members of the board were non executives who had their own companies to consider when they were in competition with EPRM. He did delegate and there is little to suggest that he did so unwisely but his decision to increase working hours on a Saturday can only be described as a blunder.

Sitting Rabbit

On the 1st June 1913 on the main gates of New Kleinfontein mine, which hitherto earned a reputation for good management and one which to the outside world treated their employees well was posted: NOTICE in terms of section 5(1) of the Industrial Disputes Prevention Act 1909 on or after the 1st July 1913 the hours of work of underground mechanics will be each working day including Saturday 7.30 am – 3.30 pm. being the same hours as underground employees. He must have known that the white unions would never stand for it. He knew that the African natives and the Chinese would welcome any opportunity to earn extra money and so he took a gamble and although followed by other mine owners it backfired spectacularly. The cartoonists had a field day depicting George as a sitting rabbit for the unions and his political adversaries to shoot at. The white unions called out the entire mine without a vote and organised marches from mine to mine exerting all to come out on strike. George knew that many of his employees were keen racegoers and followers of his colours at Turffontein. Their Saturday afternoons were precious to them. Union leaders acted swiftly.

Conversation

Railway workers were next to act. Violence came quickly. The premises of 'The Star newspaper were broken into and burnt to the ground'. Strike breakers were attacked. A General Strike was proclaimed shortly after The Federation of Trade Unions had come out in support of the miners. The mine owners agreed to withdraw the notice but the unions rejected this offer insisting that all strikers be reinstated and all 'scabs be dismissed'. Unsurprisingly the mine owners refused.

Gunsmiths were broken into and all their guns and ammunition looted. Armed gangs were roaming the streets of central Johannesburg. Newspapers chronicled each event giving a detailed account of what occurred each day. There was mob rule and the Government had to act. The Prime Minister chose to speak first with the leaders of the miners and the Federation of Trade unions. They now increased their demand to include full compensation for the period of the strike to be paid by the mine owners before they would call the strike off. George and Lionel Phillips were summoned to a meeting with The Prime Minister (Louis Botha) and Jan Smuts. The Prime Minister and George did most of the talking. The PM set out the union's demands. George agreed with some reluctance to take all the previous employees back but not to dismiss those who had stood by the company. The PM and JS appeared to believe that the union's demand was perfectly reasonable or perhaps they were simply recognising the strength of the union's bargaining position. They offered to pay half of whatever compensation would have to be paid to the scabs. At this George dug his heels in and insisted they would be entitled to a year's compensation. They wanted him to pay half but he refused to contribute anything towards it. Having received what they believed to be sufficient to persuade the unions to call off the strike they agreed that the Government would pay the compensation outlined by George. Their claim for compensation was not discussed.

During the strike on the 22nd April there was a telephone call from the city centre from an old employee to say they had heard a party saying they were going out to Bedford Farm with what the caller described as 'evil intent'. Ella was in England pregnant with my mother who was born 6 days later. George rang Miss Berry, the children's governess and tutor and without giving any reasons told her to take the children and the maids to the Farm manager's house. Cars were removed from the front of the house. He had male friends to dinner. They were each armed and in dinner jackets positioned in various positions around the house. George positioned himself at the front approach to the house. We do not know what he said or did but after a while he returned to the house and said they could resume their dinner 'they were only natives'.

The Sunday Times employed a fine cartoonist called Lloyd; George was an ever-present figure even if his diminutive frame often resulted in him being only just visible. They did make George laugh and when Lloyd left the paper George bought a collection and had them framed and put in one of the children's rooms.

In a book called 'South Africa Today', Lionel Phillips and George are contrasted: 'Sir Lionel Phillips brings to the practice of politics a clear, diplomatic intellect, a close knowledge of all South Africa's problems and a sincere anxiety to see the country become a contented, strong and prosperous part of the Empire. Sir George Farrar has identical aims but pursues them by a different path. He is a blunt speaker. Force rather than finesse is his weapon. He is untiringly industrious and will patiently 'get up' a subject to master every detail while others are still waiting to begin'.

CHAPTER 12

In the summer of 1914, he returned to England for a holiday and made a speech at his old school at Bedford. Shortly afterwards War was declared. Now 55 years of age he did not hesitate before volunteering for military service. He was due to join General Hamilton's staff with the British army in Belgium when an urgent plea came from Louis Botha for his return to South Africa, which he answered. On arrival back in South Africa George went to see Botha and in a letter to Ella revealed that he had told him that he 'would do all I can'. He said that the British Empire owed Louis Botha an enormous debt. There were only 12 followers of Hertzog, who voted against South African participation when the issue was put to parliament. George told Ella that Hertzog had a visceral hatred of Botha. In due course Hertzog would become Prime Minister right up to the outbreak of the Second World war. George will have known only too well that there were many German sympathisers among Afrikaners and a grouping, who would be engaged in acts of sabotage, but George felt total loyalty to The Union he had helped to form and returned to South Africa, where he was sent to Brigadier General Sir Duncan McKenzie's Division in German South West Africa with the rank of Lieutenant Colonel as Acting Quartermaster General. He travelled to Luderitzbucht in advance of the central invasion force in order to organise the base camp. He volunteered to be responsible for the restoration and maintenance of the railway destroyed by the Germans. He asked for and was given some of his old comrades in The Kaffrarian Rifles for this task and he was promoted to full Colonel. Locomotives, rolling stock and miles of track had to be brought from the Union by sea to complete a new railway system reconstructed to enable vital supplies, water and equipment to be transported to base camps to meet the needs of 50,000 troops. The large equipment could only be unloaded by night because of enemy reconnaissance planes making sorties overhead. George supervised and took a bottle of brandy with him from which everyone took a sip. 'It went down a treat'.

The Germans used a different gauge to that in operation throughout the Union. All 5 boreholes had been dynamited and the pumps and boilers had been damaged beyond repair. Captain Valentine, an officer who served with him recalled: 'His HQ was in a caboose (a closed in box truck) in which temperatures rose to well over 100 degrees. He slept on the floor and dined on usual camp furniture. I say he slept and ate but although I repeatedly looked in on him in the early hours and late at night, he seemed always to be awake and alert and never once did I find him having a meal. He *used* not smoked hundreds of cigarettes a day. He would ask for a cigarette, light it, blow a few puffs then throw it away. He was the terror of the lax and the indolent and was known as 'Foxy' because he was always turning up at unexpected places and moments and asking inconvenient questions. In a letter to Ella he admitted going 36 hours without sleep or respite. The heat and the dust in the desert are terrible. His name became a byword for hustle. He was the unseen energy for the Central Force. He seldom seemed to have time for a wash or a shave'. Bear in mind he is much too old to have been allowed to serve as a Colonel in the Second World War and he was doing far more active manual work than a colonel of an ordinary regiment would have done.

Another account of the work schedule reads: 'Our routine of work would commence at 5.45am. Sir George would see that we all had early morning coffee at his caboose then away out with our escort work until 9 when a halt was called for breakfast then another break for lunch at 1 and a final break to get home before sunset. Sir George always insisted that the officer in command of work dined with him when we would discuss the programme for the following day. He insisted that a contemporaneous note was made and read over to him which he would then initial. Then there would be a trip to the telephone to coordinate other works in hand and other affairs of the campaign were discussed. The weather was very taxing due to heat and the glare of the sand but Sir George's usual attire was helmet, shirt, riding breeches, leggings and boots. He always carried his field glasses and on occasions a firearm. As work progressed an endeavour was made each day to eclipse the previous day's work. We took our meals on the cattle truck on the train. We were losing much time by

Parade for visit of Gen. Louis Botha

George and Gen. Louis Botha outside George's caboose

Windswept sandy terrain of German South West
with mountains in the distance

people particularly natives stopping work to go for a drink, so Sir George insisted that everyone had their own water bottle and people were employed to come to each of us at regular intervals and fill up our water bottles'.

Another tribute from one of those working with him reads: 'The rank and file couldn't understand how a man so well off, able to command such luxury, possessor of a beautiful home (two if you count Chicheley which was rented), a happy husband and father how he could sacrifice everything and come and 'slog in' like he was doing, excited their surprise and admiration'. When told of this he responded: 'As long as I am serving my King its good enough for me'.

Another stated: 'Water was found at a depth of 120 feet. The heat was intense. It was 120 degrees in the tents and one day the thermometer registered 137 degrees and there was Sir George in his thick breeches and boots. Sand got everywhere even into the food.

Enemy aeroplanes paid regular visits and often damaged the railway line we had relaid which was soul destroying, but Sir George would often say to cheer us up: "A nation is seen at its best when it is at war"'. Sentiments which would not have sprung to the lips of his youngest brother Fred who was a conscientious objector.

On Wednesday the 19th May 1915 he motored out to Brakwasser 47 kilometres away because he wanted to investigate a suitable site for a new supply base. At 5.30 he phoned Captain Price, his staff officer, to say that he was leaving for Kulbis. Price gave this information to The Station Office at Kulbis. To whom Price spoke we do not know but when Station Master Barnes was asked to clear the line for men to take material up the line, he was unaware of any message from Price. A further call was made at 6.15 to ensure the line was still clear. Lance Corporal Botha was now acting Station Master said a train had just gone. George came into the office immediately afterwards and said: 'See if you can stop the train and let me through'. Botha tried in vain. George then said: 'I'll get off,' and left in a hurry. The words 'I'll get off' were ambivalent. I think what he meant was that he would get off the trolley, which was apparently quite light and pull it off the track and wait for the train to pass before putting it back on the track. George had always been reckless where his own life was at risk and this time the gods would not be kind. Botha did call back to say that George's orders were for the train to be delayed at Kulbis but he couldn't do that because the delay would be too long. He said Barnes would warn them if you let it come be careful to give your location warning. That conversation took place 5 minutes before the train left Kulbis at 6.33. The engine driver and the fireman did receive that warning. George's motor trolley left Brakwasser without any notice to proceed. On the trolley George was holding a lamp in his hand because it was already getting dark. Normally Lieutenant Bradley would have been sitting in front but George insisted on sitting in front presumably because he knew the inherent danger. They were entering a big curve with a 12ft. high banking on one side, which would have deadened the sound of the oncoming train. It was by now very dark. A slight drizzle had begun. The wind had increased in force blowing sand into their faces. The motor of the trolley was

Trolley after the accident

making its usual ghastly noise making it impossible to hear the approach of the train. As George jumped, he was caught on the thigh by the tank truck which preceded the engine and may not have been very visible and may well have impaired the vision of the oncoming train driver. The frenzied shouts of Fireman van Rooyen came too late. The driver applied the brakes hard and because they were not moving fast the train could stop within 30 yards. At the bottom of the embankment George was found lying on his side fully conscious with his thigh in a pool of blood. His face was very drawn as if in extreme pain. 'Leave me alone and attend to the other fellow who is hurt more than me. This thing is such a nuisance when I have so much work still to do'.

An ambulance van arrived at 9 pm and George was taken to the Station office, where he was given an anaesthetic and operated on to sever his leg at the knee. He rallied from the effects of the chloroform and after talking for a while said he felt comfortable and nodded off at 4.30 am. His pulse became feebler and he gradually lost consciousness. He died at 5.05 am. His last coherent words were: 'When we consider the conditions here a great deal has been accomplished'. This was a reference to the fact that there had been a remarkable advance of the reconstruction of the sabotaged railway from Luderitzbucht right up to the railhead. This brief account of his medical condition was made available at the time of his death. The full detailed medical reports were for some reason not publicly released until 1966 some 50 years after his death. They make no reference to an amputation but they give as one of the reasons for applying chloroform the possibility of surgical procedure. The description of the fracture is inconsistent in the two recently released reports. One describes it as 'a *compound* fracture of the thigh' and the other 'a *slight* fracture of the great trochanter'. The cause of death given (agreed by both doctors) is also surprising bearing in mind that:

1. There was only a small scalp wound to the top of the forehead.
2. No Xray was taken of the skull to which any reference is made.
3. George was perfectly coherent throughout the night only complaining of the cold and inability to move his left leg. The cause of death given was 'Shock and internal haemorrhaging due to a fracture at the base of the skull'.

One of the veterinary staff who came into close touch with George said 'From sun up to sun down George was to be seen always working and always with a kind word for anyone who needed assistance'. Probably because of the deep respect and love for George, there were some attempts later to shift the blame for this tragic accident on to other shoulders but in truth George was the sole author and would have been horrified if anyone else had been forced to share the blame.

The funeral could not take place for almost a month awaiting the arrival of Ella and Helen and Muriel who accompanied her on the Dunvegan Castle. One wonders why Gwen and Marjorie were not included. Kathleen was just nine and my mother, another Ella, just 4. Why did it take so long? Maybe the voyage then took 3 weeks with more port stops necessary for refuelling. At Madeira Ella received a cablegram from The King and Queen 'regretting the loss you and South Africa have sustained by the loss of your husband in the service of The Empire. Their majesties truly sympathise with you in your sorrow'. Ella sent a reply saying how deeply touched she was by their gracious sympathy. They docked at Cape Town in the afternoon and left for Johannesburg at 8.30 driving through the night in a special saloon provided by The Government. It is 734 miles to Johannesburg from Cape Town by road. A photograph shows the cortege of people not vehicles at the funeral going as far as the eye can see. At the funeral service at Chicheley the Basuto pony, called Wepener which had carried him throughout the Second Boer war, sometimes travelling 80 miles a day, lead the procession before returning to his stable.

There is an entire volume of tributes to him following his death. The final 3 paragraphs of his obituary in The Times recorded on 21st May 1915 are worth repeating:

'As a politician George Farrar had to a singular degree the power of endearing himself to his followers. He would go out into the street and talk to any man he met with a complete simplicity and a total absence of affectation that won all hearts. This gift came naturally to him. It laid the foundation of a great popularity, which found striking expression when he felt bound to resign his seat in Parliament.

'Simplicity of character was also the note of George Farrar as a man. In his young days at the Cape, he was a great athlete, distinguished in running and as an oar. When success came to him, he remained the same blunt, plain man he had always been; shrewd and keen in business, devoting himself without stint to public duties, but never losing his interest in outdoor recreations. His farm outside Johannesburg was very near to his heart, and nothing pleased him better than to win prizes with the cattle that he bred there. As a soldier, these qualities enabled him to do service to his country far beyond the capacity of the ordinary civilian in arms. It was characteristic of him that when the South African Government undertook the expedition against German South West Africa, he should offer himself for the humdrum but supremely important duty of organising transport.

Mrs Farrar
returns her heartfelt thanks for
kind sympathy in the
deep sorrow of the loss of her son,
Sir George Farrar, May 20,
and of her grandson,
Captain John Harold Farrar,
May 9; both killed while on
active service in the war for
their country.

The Crescent Lodge,
Bedford.

George's mother's response to condolences

Outside the Church of St Mary Magdelene, Benoni

Following the gun carriage

a) Approaching Bedford Farm b) Waiting for the coffin, which was brought indoors for a short space c) The Kaffrarian Rifles, Sir George's own regiment, in the procession in Bedford Park

Taking wreathes to the grave

Flowers by George's grave

It is said that a crowd of 6,000 attended the service
and walked just under 2 miles to the gravesite

Steps leading to George's grave

Plaque commemorating the grave

Recently restored surround to the grave

George with hands on hips with the gang
taking a break at a borehole

'Above all George Farrar was a fighter; not a fighter for the mere love of fighting but one of those who love a tight corner where they can set their teeth and endure against overwhelming odds. Set him in such a place and there could be no better man – none more loyal none more steadfast or more resolute. The arid and hostile country that guards South West Africa against invasion from the sea – the heat, its dust, its thirst, the sand – leaden, violent winds – were enemies such as his heart desired. He was never happier, we may be sure, than when he was fighting and overcoming them. His death is a loss to South Africa that can hardly be made good'.

In another part of the same edition under the heading of 'Sir George Farrar' is another article which reads:

'The brilliant little campaign in South West Africa – so far the most completely successful of all our worldwide operations – has cost the life of a man to whom its success has been very largely due. As the

Prime Minister explained in his speech at Guildhall on Wednesday: "the essential difficulties of the advance to Windhoek lay in questions of transport and supply. A long sea voyage, a strip of waterless desert, a country almost devoid of roads and railways, an enemy who resorted to every diabolical device of poison and infection – these are some of the conditions with which General Botha's forces have been confronted during the last few months; and his chief lieutenant in conquering them has been Sir George Farrar. Now at the very moment of accomplishment Sir George Farrar has been killed in the service of his country – just as truly as if he had fallen on the actual field of battle – and South Africa and the whole Empire are the poorer for his death ... Sir George Farrar was at once the head of a great industry, a reformer – one of the four who were sentenced to death, a distinguished soldier in the South African war and a leader of a political party since the peace. Unlike too many South African 'magnates', he gave the best of his life to the country where he had made his name and fortune. He worked hard for the Union and it is a fitting crown to his career and the death he would have chosen, that he should have fallen in face of the enemy with a triumphant and united force of both South African races". This final remark will stick in the craw today but I think it is fair to point out that everyone appears to be working together in a joint enterprise and native Africans were included in joint photographs, which would certainly not have been the case years later'.

On the same day May 21st all the mining offices and Stock and Commercial exchanges closed as a mark of respect to Sir George Farrar.

Writing after the funeral F.S. (unidentified) wrote:

'Farrar like Rhodes was essentially a simple man and a worker. If his horizon was not so far flung that was because his opportunities were not so great. He made South Africa his home and built for himself out in the Bezuidenhout valley a house of elegance surrounding it with appurtenances of a country estate rather than a farm as we know farming in this land. Visitors to his grave will watch from rugged ridges beneath which his body lies the estate of Bedford Farm grow richer and more beautiful as the seasons roll by. They will see the trees

Garden in front of Bedford Farm

which he planted ennoble the homestead and grandchildren coming from time to time to that spot, which must ever be sacred to them'.

In 1968 the Town Council of Benoni issued a full-scale map of their town on the front of which was a portrait of Sir George Farrar. One of the two joint authors was Deryck Humphriss referred to above, an old boy of Bedford Modern School, George's old school in England. George had personally designed and planned the older part of Benoni naming streets after his family and familiar names of Bedfordshire origin hence Ampthill Avenue, Bedford Avenue, Bunyan Street, Howard Avenue, Newport Pagnell, Turvey Street and Woburn Avenue. A recently extended suburb is named 'Farrarmere'. His house, Bedford, has become St Andrew's School. Lady Farrar's boudoir now serves as the Standard VI Common room. The bedrooms of the Farrar daughters are now the bedrooms of members of staff and senior girls.

George is buried on an outcrop overlooking the farm.

POSTSCRIPT

The material used has all been taken from contemporaneous newspaper accounts; personal correspondence and my aunt Muriel's personal memoirs and a thick book of jottings written by his personal secretary H. Webber, all of which are lodged in The Farrar archives in The Weston library (part of The Bodleian) in Oxford. The Farrar Archives are a collection of contemporaneous papers recording the life of Sir George Farrar in the possession of George Turner eldest son of Helen Turner (Sir George's eldest daughter), James Earl of Lonsdale, eldest son of Muriel Viscountess Lowther (Sir George's second daughter) and Ella Lady Watson (Sir George's youngest daughter). They were presented to the Bodleian Library by James Earl of Lonsdale in December 1994. There is no corroboration for the account of the running challenge of George and the fastest African. It is something I was told by my aunt Helen. It is certainly curious that there is no mention of it elsewhere, but it is a surprising fact for her to have invented.

Milton Keynes UK
Ingram Content Group UK Ltd.
UKHW020629140923
428661UK00004B/23

9 781803 812816